# Chasing Legends: The Truth behind the Loch Ness Monster

Oliver Lancaster

Published by Oliver Lancaster, 2023.

While every precaution has been taken in the preparation of this book, the publisher assumes no responsibility for errors or omissions, or for damages resulting from the use of the information contained herein.

CHASING LEGENDS: THE TRUTH BEHIND THE LOCH NESS MONSTER

**First edition. July 14, 2023.**



ISBN: 979-8223776758

Written by Oliver Lancaster.

# Also by Oliver Lancaster

Chernobyl: Unveiling the tragedy. A Comprehensive Account of the Nuclear Disaster

The Bhopal Gas Tragedy: Unraveling the Catastrophe of 1984

The Deepwater Horizon Oil Spill of 2010: A Disaster Unveiled

Fukushima Fallout: Unveiling the Truth behind the 2011 Nuclear Disaster

Minamata Disease: Poisoned Waters and the Battle for Justice (1932-1968)

Evil Women: Unmasking History's Most Notorious Women

Bundy The Dark Chronicles: America's Infamous Serial Killer

Dahmer The Dark Chronicles: America's Infamous Milwaukee Cannibal

Zodiac The Dark Chronicles: America's Infamous Cryptic Killer

Bigfoot: The Comprehensive Investigation into the Elusive Legend

Chasing Legends: The Truth behind the Chupacabra

Chasing Legends: The Truth behind the Loch Ness Monster

Watch for more at https://tinyurl.com/olanc.

Sign up to my free newsletter to get updates on new releases, FREE teaser chapters to upcoming releases and FREE digital short stories.

Or visit https://tinyurl.com/olanc

I never spam and you can unsubscribe at any time.

# OLIVER LANCASTER

## Disclaimer

The information presented in this book is based on historical accounts, scientific research, and eyewitness testimonies. While every effort has been made to provide accurate and up-to-date information, the author and publisher make no claims regarding the existence or non-existence of the Loch Ness Monster. The opinions and theories presented are those of the respective individuals and do not necessarily reflect the views of the author or publisher. This book is intended for entertainment purposes and to foster curiosity about the mysteries of the Loch Ness Monster. Readers are encouraged to explore further research and draw their own conclusions.

# Chasing Legends: The Truth behind the Loch Ness Monster

# OLIVER LANCASTER

# Chapter 1: Introduction

The Loch Ness Monster, often affectionately referred to as "Nessie," is a legendary creature said to inhabit the deep waters of Loch Ness, a large freshwater lake located in the Scottish Highlands. With a history spanning centuries, the Loch Ness Monster has captured the imagination and curiosity of people worldwide, becoming one of the most enduring and famous cryptids.

The first recorded sighting of the Loch Ness Monster can be traced back to the year 565 AD, when the Irish monk Saint Columba allegedly encountered a fearsome water beast in the River Ness. According to the account, Saint Columba managed to scare off the creature by making the sign of the cross and invoking the name of God. This encounter marked the earliest known mention of a mysterious creature lurking in the waters of Loch Ness.

Fast forward to the 20th century, and the modern legend of the Loch Ness Monster truly began to take shape. In the early 1930s, a series of reported sightings by local residents and visitors to Loch Ness garnered widespread attention in the media, catapulting Nessie into the realm of popular culture. Eyewitness testimonies described a large aquatic creature with a long neck and humps, occasionally surfacing and then disappearing into the depths, leaving behind a trail of mystery.

The Loch Ness Monster quickly became a subject of fascination and speculation, attracting not only curious locals but also scientists, explorers, and skeptics eager to unravel the truth behind the legend. Numerous expeditions were organized, utilizing state-of-the-art technology and innovative methods to search for evidence of Nessie's existence.

As the legend grew, Loch Ness became a magnet for tourists and monster enthusiasts from around the world. The lure of a potential encounter with this enigmatic creature turned the picturesque Scottish Highlands into a hub of excitement and anticipation. Books, documentaries, and films dedicated to the Loch Ness Monster proliferated, fueling the public's imagination and perpetuating the enduring mystery.

Over the years, several photographs and videos claiming to capture the elusive creature have emerged, each sparking debates and controversy. The most famous of these is the "Surgeon's Photograph" taken by Robert Kenneth Wilson in 1934, which portrayed what appeared to be a long-necked creature rising from the water. While initially celebrated as concrete evidence of the monster's existence, the photograph was later revealed to be a hoax, tarnishing its credibility.

Despite the lack of irrefutable evidence, the allure of the Loch Ness Monster endures. Scientists continue to investigate the lake's depths, employing advanced sonar, underwater cameras, and other technological advancements in their quest to unlock the secrets hidden beneath the surface. Each new expedition brings hope that one day, the truth behind the Loch Ness

# CHASING LEGENDS: THE TRUTH BEHIND THE LOCH NESS MONSTER

Monster will be revealed, either confirming its existence or dispelling it as nothing more than a fascinating myth.

As we delve deeper into the pages of this book, we will embark on a journey to separate fact from fiction, exploring the various theories put forth by experts, analyzing eyewitness accounts, and examining the scientific research conducted over the years. Together, we will unravel the enigma that is the Loch Ness Monster and seek to uncover the truth that lies beneath the rippling waters of Loch Ness.

The purpose of this book, "Chasing Legends: The Truth behind the Loch Ness Monster," is to embark on a comprehensive exploration of the various theories and evidence surrounding the existence of the creature that has captivated the imagination of countless individuals for centuries. Through meticulous research, analysis of eyewitness accounts, and examination of scientific investigations, we aim to shed light on the enduring mystery of the Loch Ness Monster.

Throughout history, numerous theories have emerged in an attempt to explain the Loch Ness Monster phenomenon. Some believe that Nessie is a remnant of prehistoric creatures, a surviving dinosaur or marine reptile that somehow eluded extinction. Others propose that the monster is a unique species yet undiscovered by science, possibly an ancient aquatic reptile or an unidentified marine mammal. A third line of thought suggests that the sightings are misidentifications of more mundane objects or phenomena, such as floating logs, waves, or large fish.

To unravel the truth, we will delve into each of these theories, examining their strengths and weaknesses, while also considering alternative explanations. We will consult experts in fields such as marine biology, cryptozoology, and psychology to gain insights into the plausibility of the various hypotheses. By carefully weighing the evidence and scrutinizing the accounts of eyewitnesses, we will strive to separate fact from fiction and present a balanced and objective assessment.

The Loch Ness Monster has been the subject of extensive scientific investigations over the years. Numerous expeditions and research projects have sought to employ cutting-edge technology to scan the murky depths of Loch Ness, employing sonar, underwater cameras, and advanced imaging techniques. By examining the results of these studies, we can evaluate the scientific rigor behind the search for Nessie and assess the validity of any evidence that has been put forward.

Eyewitness accounts play a crucial role in the lore of the Loch Ness Monster. People from all walks of life have reported sightings and encounters with the creature, providing valuable testimonies that contribute to the ongoing debate. In this book, we will analyze these accounts, considering factors such as the reliability of witnesses, the consistency of descriptions, and the potential for misinterpretation or exaggeration.

Additionally, we will explore the cultural and psychological aspects surrounding the Loch Ness Monster. The creature's enduring popularity and its impact on the local economy and tourism industry raise intriguing questions about the human fascination with mythical beasts. We will delve into the psychological underpinnings of belief in cryptids and examine how folklore and legend intertwine with scientific inquiry.

Ultimately, the purpose of this book is not to provide a definitive answer regarding the existence of the Loch Ness Monster, but rather to present readers with a comprehensive and objective exploration of the subject. By considering the diverse theories, scrutinizing the evidence, and analyzing the cultural and scientific context, we hope to stimulate critical thinking and encourage readers to form their own informed opinions on this enduring mystery.

Next, we will delve into the history of sightings, investigate the scientific expeditions and research, and explore the potential explanations and implications of the Loch Ness Monster phenomenon. Join us on this captivating journey as we seek to uncover the truth behind the legend and separate fact from fiction in the enigmatic realm of Nessie, the Loch Ness Monster.

# OLIVER LANCASTER

# Chapter 2: Mythology and Folklore

The shores of Loch Ness have long been steeped in a rich tapestry of mythology and folklore, woven together with tales of the Loch Ness Monster. These stories have been passed down through generations, adding to the allure and mystery surrounding the legendary creature.

The origins of Loch Ness's mythology can be traced back centuries, intertwined with the ancient Celtic traditions and beliefs of the Scottish Highlands. The loch itself holds a special place in Scottish folklore, believed to be inhabited by magical beings and spirits. Water creatures, known as kelpies, were said to lure unsuspecting travelers into the depths with their mesmerizing songs. Such tales set the stage for the emergence of the Loch Ness Monster as a larger-than-life figure in local folklore.

One of the most prevalent legends associated with the Loch Ness Monster is that of the Water Horse, or "each-uisge" in Scottish Gaelic. The Water Horse was believed to be a shapeshifting creature that could transform into a horse or a beautiful young man, enticing people to ride on its back. However, once mounted, the creature would plunge into the water, drowning its victim. This cautionary tale served as a warning to those who dared to venture too close to the mysterious waters of Loch Ness.

Another prominent figure in Loch Ness folklore is the Blue Men of the Minch, who were thought to be mythical beings inhabiting the waters between the Outer Hebrides and the Scottish mainland. These semi-divine creatures were said to possess the ability to control the waves and winds, appearing as blue-skinned men with long beards. The tales of the Blue Men resonated with the Loch Ness Monster mythology, further fueling the belief in the existence of supernatural creatures dwelling in the depths.

As the modern legend of the Loch Ness Monster began to take shape in the early 20th century, it intertwined with the existing folklore of the region, capturing the imagination of locals and tourists alike. Stories of encounters with Nessie became an integral part of Highland lore, with eyewitness testimonies and local anecdotes adding layers of intrigue to the mythos. Loch Ness became a pilgrimage site for those seeking a glimpse of the mysterious creature, and the tales of their experiences became part of the ongoing narrative.

Over time, Loch Ness folklore has become intertwined with popular culture and media representations. Books, films, and television shows have embraced the legend of the Loch Ness Monster, further perpetuating its mythical status. The iconic image of a long-necked creature rising from the dark waters has become deeply ingrained in popular consciousness, transcending geographical boundaries and captivating the global imagination.

However, it is essential to distinguish between folklore and the scientific investigation of the Loch Ness Monster. While folklore provides a rich cultural backdrop and offers insights into the collective beliefs and imagination of a community, scientific inquiry seeks to analyze the evidence and establish empirical facts. The interplay between folklore and scientific exploration is a fascinating aspect of the Loch Ness Monster phenomenon, highlighting the complex relationship between tradition, myth, and the quest for truth.

Next, we will further explore the fascinating intersection of folklore and scientific investigation. We will examine how the rich mythology surrounding the Loch Ness Monster has shaped public perceptions, fueled curiosity, and influenced the ongoing search for answers. Join us as we unravel the layers of folklore and delve deeper into the enigmatic world of Nessie, where ancient tales merge with modern quests for truth.

Scotland, with its breathtaking landscapes and rich cultural heritage, has a wealth of ancient legends and tales related to water creatures. These mythical beings have fascinated and intrigued people for centuries, casting an ethereal veil over the country's lakes, rivers, and lochs. In this section, we will explore some of the most captivating Scottish legends and delve into the enchanting realm of water creatures that inhabit the folklore of this land.

One of the most well-known figures in Scottish mythology is the selkie, a creature that is said to possess the ability to transform between a seal and a human form. Legends speak of selkies as beautiful, graceful beings who would shed their seal skins to reveal their true human selves. It is believed that they would come ashore to bask in the moonlight or to seek human companionship. Tales often revolve around the captivating love stories between selkies and mortals, where the humans either unknowingly or willingly fall in love with these mysterious creatures of the sea.

Similar to selkies, the ceasg, or the Highland mermaid, is another intriguing water creature in Scottish folklore. These beings were depicted as half-human and half-fish, with a human-like upper body and a fish-like lower body. The ceasg was known for its mesmerizing voice, which it would use to lure unsuspecting travelers or fishermen into the depths of the water. In some tales, they were considered benevolent beings, bestowing gifts upon those who treated them kindly.

Kelpies, often associated with Scottish lochs and rivers, are legendary water horses or water spirits that were said to reside near bodies of water. These creatures would often appear as beautiful horses, enticing people to ride on their backs. However, once mounted, the kelpies' true nature would be revealed, as they would drag their victims into the water, drowning them. The tales of the kelpies served as cautionary warnings about the dangers lurking in the depths and the unpredictable nature of water.

The Each-uisge, or Water Horse, is another prominent water creature in Scottish mythology. Known for its shapeshifting abilities, the Each-uisge could take the form of a beautiful horse, tempting people to ride it. However, once mounted, the creature's skin would become adhesive, trapping the rider. It would then gallop into the water, drowning its unfortunate victim. These tales served as warnings about the treacherous nature of the lochs and rivers, emphasizing the need for caution and respect.

Scottish folklore is also replete with stories of water spirits known as nixies or water nymphs. These beings were believed to inhabit pools, streams, and waterfalls, captivating passersby with their beauty and enchanting melodies. They were known for their mischievous nature, luring unsuspecting individuals into the water or seducing them with their mesmerizing voices. However, nixies could also be benevolent, offering protection and good fortune to those who treated them with kindness and respect.

These ancient Scottish legends and tales of water creatures provide a glimpse into the deep connection between the Scottish people and their natural surroundings. They embody a reverence for the power and mystery of water, highlighting the delicate balance between fascination and caution when encountering these otherworldly beings. These legends continue to be passed down through generations, enriching the cultural fabric of Scotland and adding to the allure of its majestic landscapes.

Next, we will explore how these ancient legends intertwine with the mythos of the Loch Ness Monster, contributing to the collective imagination surrounding the enigmatic creature. Join us as we delve further into the realms of folklore and uncover the mystical threads that connect the ancient tales of water creatures to the enduring legend of Nessie, the Loch Ness Monster.

# OLIVER LANCASTER

# Chapter 3: Geological and Historical Background

To truly understand the mysteries that surround the Loch Ness Monster, it is crucial to delve into the geological formation of Loch Ness itself. This expansive body of water holds significant scientific and historical importance, shaping the landscape of the Scottish Highlands and providing the stage upon which the legend of Nessie unfolds.

Loch Ness is a freshwater loch located in the Great Glen, a dramatic geological fault line that stretches from Fort William in the west to Inverness in the east. It is the second largest loch in Scotland by surface area, measuring approximately 37 kilometers (23 miles) long and 1.6 kilometers (1 mile) wide. With a maximum depth of 230 meters (754 feet), it holds more water than all the lakes in England and Wales combined.

The formation of Loch Ness can be attributed to the retreat of glaciers during the last Ice Age, which occurred approximately 10,000 years ago. As colossal sheets of ice carved their way through the Scottish Highlands, they left behind a trail of glacial valleys, or "glens," and deep trenches. These trenches filled with meltwater and ultimately formed the lochs that grace the Scottish landscape today, including Loch Ness.

The surrounding geology of Loch Ness is predominantly composed of ancient rocks, with the Great Glen Fault acting as a significant geological feature. This fault line, created by tectonic forces, extends across the length of Scotland, representing a zone of weakness in the Earth's crust. It is responsible for the creation of the Great Glen and the formation of several other lochs along its path.

The geological significance of Loch Ness goes beyond its formation. The loch's depth and size make it an essential source of freshwater for the region, supporting a diverse ecosystem of plants and animals. Its deep, dark waters, influenced by the surrounding peat bogs, give rise to unique environmental conditions that contribute to its allure and mystery.

The geological features of Loch Ness have also played a role in shaping the legend of the Loch Ness Monster. The deep trenches, hidden caves, and underwater ledges create a vast and complex underwater terrain, providing ample hiding places for any creature that might reside there. These geological characteristics have fueled speculation about the existence of hidden passages or underground tunnels within the loch, potentially offering an explanation for how the Loch Ness Monster could evade detection.

Moreover, the geological importance of Loch Ness extends to its cultural and historical significance. The loch and its surroundings have been inhabited by humans for thousands of years, with evidence of ancient settlements and archaeological sites dating back to the Bronze Age. The iconic Urquhart Castle, overlooking the loch, stands as a testament to the area's rich history and the strategic importance of Loch Ness as a defensive stronghold.

# CHASING LEGENDS: THE TRUTH BEHIND THE LOCH NESS MONSTER

Today, Loch Ness continues to draw visitors from around the world, intrigued by its natural beauty and the allure of the Loch Ness Monster. The loch's geological formation and its connection to ancient times provide a backdrop for the ongoing exploration and scientific investigation into the mysteries that lie beneath its surface.

Next, we will explore the scientific research conducted in Loch Ness, examining how its geological features have influenced the search for evidence of the Loch Ness Monster. By understanding the geological significance of Loch Ness, we gain a deeper appreciation for the enigmatic nature of this iconic Scottish landmark and the enduring quest to unravel its secrets.

The legend of the Loch Ness Monster has not only captured the imaginations of people worldwide but has also become deeply intertwined with the historical events and cultural context surrounding Loch Ness and the Scottish Highlands. In this section, we will explore the significant historical events and cultural factors that have shaped the Loch Ness Monster legend and contributed to its enduring popularity.

The origins of the Loch Ness Monster legend can be traced back to early accounts and folklore that permeated the Scottish Highlands. Tales of water creatures and mythical beasts were part of the rich oral tradition passed down through generations, setting the stage for the emergence of the Loch Ness Monster as a prominent figure in local folklore.

One of the most notable events in the history of the Loch Ness Monster legend is the famous "Surgeon's Photograph" taken in 1934 by Robert Kenneth Wilson. This photograph, depicting what appeared to be a long-necked creature rising from the water, garnered worldwide attention and solidified Nessie's place in popular culture. Although the photograph was later revealed to be a hoax, its impact on the Loch Ness Monster's legend was substantial.

The Loch Ness Monster legend gained widespread media coverage and became a subject of fascination in the mid-20th century. Newspapers, magazines, and radio broadcasts fueled the public's imagination, attracting tourists and monster enthusiasts from around the world. Loch Ness became a popular destination, and the local economy boomed with the influx of visitors eager to catch a glimpse of Nessie.

The scientific community has also played a significant role in the Loch Ness Monster's legend. Numerous expeditions and research projects have been conducted over the years, employing advanced sonar technology, underwater cameras, and other scientific methods to search for evidence of the creature's existence. These scientific efforts have both added to the allure of the legend and prompted critical scrutiny of the evidence.

The Loch Ness Monster has become an iconic symbol of Scotland, its folklore, and its natural beauty. The creature's image is deeply ingrained in popular culture, appearing in books, films, and various forms of media. Nessie merchandise, such as toys, T-shirts, and souvenirs, has become a thriving industry, highlighting the creature's enduring appeal and cultural significance.

The Loch Ness Monster legend has also contributed to the conservation efforts surrounding Loch Ness and its ecosystem. The desire to protect the habitat of a potential unknown creature has spurred environmental initiatives, promoting the preservation of the loch's natural environment and the species that call it home.

Alongside the fascination and belief in the Loch Ness Monster, skepticism and debunking efforts have also shaped the legend. Many skeptics have sought to provide rational explanations for reported sightings, attributing them to misidentifications, hoaxes, or natural phenomena. These skeptical perspectives have added a critical lens to the ongoing exploration of the Loch Ness Monster phenomenon.

The historical events and cultural context surrounding the Loch Ness Monster legend have contributed to its enduring popularity and the ongoing intrigue surrounding the creature. The interplay between historical events, media coverage, scientific research, and cultural significance has woven a complex tapestry that continues to captivate the imaginations of people worldwide.

Next, we will delve deeper into the historical accounts, scientific investigations, and cultural impact surrounding the Loch Ness Monster. By exploring these facets, we aim to gain a comprehensive understanding of the legend and shed light on the truths, myths, and ongoing mysteries that surround Nessie, the enigmatic creature of Loch Ness.

24

# CHASING LEGENDS: THE TRUTH BEHIND THE LOCH NESS MONSTER

# Chapter 4: The First Sightings

The earliest recorded sightings of the Loch Ness Monster can be traced back to ancient accounts and folklore that have been passed down through the generations. While these early stories may lack specific details or scientific scrutiny, they serve as the foundation upon which the modern legend of the Loch Ness Monster is built. In this section, we will explore some of the earliest recorded sightings that have contributed to the enduring fascination with Nessie.

One of the earliest recorded sightings of a mysterious creature in the waters of Loch Ness dates back to 565 AD. According to the account, the Irish monk Saint Columba was traveling near the River Ness when he came across local residents burying a man who had been attacked and killed by a water beast. Saint Columba, known for his legendary powers, ordered one of his followers to swim across the river. As the creature approached, Saint Columba made the sign of the cross, invoking the name of God, and commanded the creature to "go no further." The creature allegedly obeyed and retreated, leaving the inhabitants in awe and reinforcing the belief in a fearsome water beast inhabiting the loch.

In 1680, Martin Martin, a Scottish writer and traveler, recorded an account of a creature encountered in Loch Ness during his explorations. He described seeing a large creature with "a long, piked snout" and a "mane of grey hair" that swam rapidly through the water. Martin's account provided early written documentation of a mysterious creature in Loch Ness, further fueling curiosity about its existence.

In 1871, D. Mackenzie, a gamekeeper at the time, witnessed a strange sighting while out on the loch. He reported seeing a large creature with a long neck, a snout resembling that of a pike, and flippers. According to his account, the creature was swimming leisurely and disappeared into the depths when it sensed his presence. This sighting attracted local attention and marked one of the first documented reports of a creature resembling the descriptions associated with the Loch Ness Monster.

Perhaps one of the most intriguing early sightings occurred in 1933 when George Spicer and his wife claimed to have encountered a large creature while driving along the loch. They reported seeing an animal with a long neck, which they estimated to be about 1.8 meters (6 feet) in height, crossing the road before entering the water. This account, widely publicized in newspapers, sparked a surge of interest and marked the beginning of the modern era of the Loch Ness Monster legend.

These early recorded sightings laid the groundwork for the emergence of the Loch Ness Monster as a significant cultural phenomenon. While these accounts vary in detail and credibility, they hold historical significance as the earliest documented reports of encounters with an elusive and mysterious creature inhabiting the waters of Loch Ness. These sightings set the stage for subsequent investigations, scientific expeditions, and the enduring quest to unravel the truth behind the legend of Nessie.

Next, we will delve deeper into the historical and scientific investigations, exploring eyewitness testimonies, and examining the evidence put forth in the ongoing search for answers. Join us as we journey further into the mysteries and complexities of the Loch Ness Monster phenomenon, seeking to separate fact from fiction in the quest for the truth behind Nessie's existence.

The early recorded sightings of the Loch Ness Monster have played a crucial role in shaping the legend and captivating the public's imagination. However, it is important to analyze the credibility of these accounts and understand their impact on the enduring fascination with the Loch Ness Monster. In this section, we will examine the credibility of these early sightings and their influence on the legend.

The account of Saint Columba's encounter with a water beast in the River Ness carries significant historical and cultural weight. As a revered figure in Scottish history, Saint Columba's story lends an air of credibility to the existence of a creature in the area. However, given the passage of time and the lack of detailed information, it is challenging to evaluate the accuracy and reliability of this account. It is important to recognize that this early tale provided a foundation for the belief in a fearsome creature inhabiting the loch, but its direct connection to the modern concept of the Loch Ness Monster is debatable.

Martin Martin's description of a creature in Loch Ness adds another layer to the evolving legend. While Martin was a reputable figure and his account is documented, the details provided are limited. Without further corroborating evidence or additional eyewitness testimonies, it is difficult to assess the accuracy and credibility of his description. Nonetheless, his account contributes to the growing body of evidence that people have observed something unusual in Loch Ness over the centuries.

The sighting reported by D. Mackenzie, a gamekeeper in 1871, provides a more detailed description of a creature resembling the Loch Ness Monster. His firsthand encounter lends some credibility to the account, as he was a local resident familiar with the area. However, like other early sightings, the lack of photographic or scientific evidence makes it challenging to validate or dismiss his report definitively. Nevertheless, this sighting, along with others, continued to spark curiosity and bolster the growing legend of Nessie.

The 1933 sighting by George Spicer and his wife is often cited as a turning point in the Loch Ness Monster legend. Their encounter, reported in the media, garnered significant attention and generated widespread interest. While the Spicer account captured public imagination, its credibility is often questioned due to the lack of photographic evidence and the potential for misinterpretation or exaggeration. Nonetheless, their sighting served as a catalyst, sparking a surge of curiosity and public fascination with the Loch Ness Monster.

# CHASING LEGENDS: THE TRUTH BEHIND THE LOCH NESS MONSTER

The impact of these early accounts on the legend of the Loch Ness Monster cannot be understated. They provided the basis for subsequent reports, investigations, and scientific inquiries. Each sighting contributed to the growing body of lore and folklore surrounding the creature, creating a captivating narrative that captured the public's imagination. The media coverage and public interest surrounding these accounts further solidified the Loch Ness Monster's place in popular culture, turning the search for Nessie into a global phenomenon.

While the credibility of these early sightings may be debated, their impact on the legend cannot be disregarded. They set the stage for the ongoing exploration, scientific investigations, and public fascination with the Loch Ness Monster. The accounts served as building blocks, establishing a foundation for further research and inspiring generations to seek answers to the mysteries that lie beneath the waters of Loch Ness.

Next, we will delve into the scientific investigations, eyewitness testimonies, and cultural impact surrounding the Loch Ness Monster. By examining the evolving body of evidence and the interplay between belief, skepticism, and scientific inquiry, we strive to uncover the truths, dispel the myths, and shed light on the enigmatic legend of Nessie.

OLIVER LANCASTER

32

# Chapter 5: Surge in Sightings

In the history of the Loch Ness Monster legend, there have been distinct periods characterized by increased sightings and heightened public interest. These periods of fascination with the creature have left an indelible mark on the Loch Ness Monster's legend, shaping its trajectory and further fueling the ongoing quest for the truth. In this section, we will explore the period of increased sightings and public interest that solidified the Loch Ness Monster's place in popular culture.

The 1930s marked a turning point in the Loch Ness Monster phenomenon, as a series of reported sightings captured the public's attention and ignited a surge of interest in the creature. It was during this time that the Loch Ness Monster transitioned from local folklore to a global fascination. Several notable sightings contributed to this period of increased interest.

The sighting reported by George Spicer and his wife in July 1933, where they described seeing a creature with a long neck crossing the road, garnered significant media coverage. This sighting, followed by the account of Arthur Grant, who claimed to have seen a large creature with a small head and a long neck, led to heightened public curiosity and speculation about the existence of a mysterious creature in Loch Ness.

One of the most iconic and controversial events in the Loch Ness Monster's history occurred in 1934 with the publication of the Surgeon's Photograph. Captured by Robert Kenneth Wilson, this photograph depicted what appeared to be a long-necked creature rising from the water. The image garnered worldwide attention, becoming the most famous photograph associated with the Loch Ness Monster at the time. Although it was later revealed to be a hoax, the Surgeon's Photograph solidified Nessie's place in popular culture and triggered a surge of public interest and speculation.

In 1960, Tim Dinsdale captured a film that purportedly showed a large, unidentified creature moving through the water. The Dinsdale Film added another layer of intrigue to the Loch Ness Monster's legend, reigniting public interest and inspiring further exploration. While skeptics questioned the film's authenticity, it contributed to the ongoing fascination and debate surrounding the creature's existence.

During the 1970s, an interesting development occurred when a cast of what was claimed to be a Loch Ness Monster's footprint was discovered. The footprint, known as the "Dobie Footprint," created a buzz of excitement and garnered media attention. However, subsequent analysis raised doubts about its authenticity, leading to further scrutiny of evidence related to the Loch Ness Monster.

These notable sightings and events during the period of increased sightings and public interest solidified the Loch Ness Monster's status as a global phenomenon. Media coverage, scientific expeditions, and the proliferation of books and documentaries further propelled the Loch Ness Monster into the public consciousness. Loch Ness became a tourist destination, attracting visitors from around the world who were eager to catch a glimpse of Nessie and be part of the ongoing search for the truth.

This period of heightened sightings and public interest had a profound impact on the Loch Ness Monster legend. It firmly established Nessie as an icon of mystery and intrigue, transcending cultural boundaries and captivating the imaginations of people worldwide. The creature became deeply ingrained in popular culture, inspiring a multitude of books, films, and merchandise.

Next, we will delve deeper into the scientific investigations, cultural impact, and ongoing search for evidence surrounding the Loch Ness Monster. By exploring the interplay between belief, skepticism, and scientific inquiry, we strive to unravel the complexities of the legend and shed light on the enduring fascination with Nessie, the enigmatic creature of Loch Ness.

Throughout the history of the Loch Ness Monster legend, numerous eyewitnesses have come forward with accounts of their encounters with the elusive creature. These testimonies have played a significant role in fueling public fascination and furthering the ongoing debate about the existence of the Loch Ness Monster. In this section, we will explore some notable eyewitness testimonies that have left an indelible mark on the legend.

Hugh Gray, a water bailiff, claimed to have witnessed a strange creature in Loch Ness in 1933. According to his account, he saw a large, dark object moving in the water, creating a considerable disturbance. Gray observed the creature for a few minutes before it submerged and disappeared. His testimony, reported in the local media, added to the growing public interest and set the stage for subsequent sightings.

Colonel Robert Kenneth Wilson is widely known for his association with the infamous Surgeon's Photograph. In 1934, Wilson claimed to have captured an image of the Loch Ness Monster, showing a long-necked creature rising from the water. The photograph gained international attention, becoming one of the most iconic images associated with Nessie. While it was later revealed to be a hoax, the photograph and Wilson's testimony had a profound impact on public perception and fueled the media frenzy surrounding the creature.

Tim Dinsdale, a British aeronautical engineer, filmed what he believed to be the Loch Ness Monster in 1960. The Dinsdale Film showed a large, hump-like object moving through the water. Dinsdale's eyewitness account and the film sparked renewed interest in the Loch Ness Monster and prompted further investigations. Despite skepticism and debates regarding the film's authenticity, Dinsdale's testimony contributed to the ongoing exploration and public fascination with Nessie.

Robert Rines, an American lawyer and inventor, dedicated decades to researching the Loch Ness Monster. Rines claimed to have captured sonar images and underwater photographs of what he believed to be the creature. His testimonies, along with the purported evidence, generated media attention and fueled the debate about the existence of Nessie. Rines' efforts added a scientific perspective to the quest for evidence and contributed to the ongoing intrigue surrounding the creature.

The Loch Ness Monster has been a magnet for media attention and a subject of intense fascination. The notable eyewitness testimonies and reported sightings have often triggered media frenzies, with newspapers, magazines, and television outlets eagerly covering the latest developments. The media frenzy surrounding the Loch Ness Monster has had a profound impact on the legend, shaping public perception and fueling the ongoing curiosity about the creature's existence.

The Surgeon's Photograph, in particular, created a media sensation when it was published in 1934. Newspapers around the world picked up the story, sparking widespread interest and speculation. The photograph became the iconic image associated with the Loch Ness Monster, propelling the legend into the global consciousness and generating a frenzy of media coverage.

Over the years, the media has played a pivotal role in reporting eyewitness accounts, scientific expeditions, and new evidence related to the Loch Ness Monster. Each reported sighting or development has been met with a surge of media attention, propelling the creature and the search for its existence into the public spotlight. Television programs, documentaries, and books dedicated to the Loch Ness Monster have further amplified the media frenzy and perpetuated the legend.

However, the media frenzy has not been without controversy. Skeptics argue that media sensationalism and the desire for attention have contributed to the proliferation of hoaxes, misidentifications, and exaggerated claims. The intense media scrutiny has also placed a spotlight on individuals making extraordinary claims, leading to questions about credibility and the reliability of eyewitness testimonies.

Nonetheless, the media frenzy has played a vital role in keeping the Loch Ness Monster legend alive and capturing the public's imagination. The constant stream of reports, discussions, and debates has ensured that the creature remains a subject of fascination, fueling ongoing interest and prompting new investigations.

Next, we will delve deeper into the scientific investigations, cultural impact, and the interplay between belief and skepticism surrounding the Loch Ness Monster. By examining the evidence and analyzing the media coverage, we aim to separate fact from fiction and shed light on the enduring mystery of Nessie, the enigmatic creature of Loch Ness.

# CHASING LEGENDS: THE TRUTH BEHIND THE LOCH NESS MONSTER

# Chapter 6: The Famous Photographs

Over the years, several photographs associated with the Loch Ness Monster have captured the public's imagination and become iconic representations of the legend. These images have fueled speculation, inspired debates, and left a lasting impact on the perception of Nessie. In this section, we will examine some of the most notable and iconic photographs associated with the Loch Ness Monster, including the infamous "Surgeon's Photograph."

The Surgeon's Photograph is perhaps the most widely recognized and controversial image linked to the Loch Ness Monster. Taken by Robert Kenneth Wilson in 1934, this photograph depicts a long-necked creature rising from the water, creating ripples around it. The image gained international attention and became synonymous with the Loch Ness Monster. However, it was later revealed to be a hoax orchestrated by Wilson and his accomplices, using a model constructed from a toy submarine with a crafted neck and head. Despite its fraudulent nature, the Surgeon's Photograph left an indelible mark on the legend and solidified Nessie's place in popular culture.

The Loch Ness Investigation Bureau (LNIB), founded in 1962, conducted various expeditions and investigations to gather evidence of the Loch Ness Monster's existence. During their efforts, the LNIB captured several photographs that gained attention in Loch Ness Monster lore. Notably, the 1963 LNIB photograph taken by F.W. Holiday shows what appears to be a large, hump-like object protruding from the water. While the photograph sparked intrigue, it remains subject to interpretation and skepticism.

The Dinsdale Film, shot by Tim Dinsdale in 1960, captured a brief yet tantalizing glimpse of a large, hump-like object moving through the water of Loch Ness. Although the film footage itself is more widely known, a still from the film showing the alleged creature has become an iconic image associated with the Loch Ness Monster. The Dinsdale Film still added a visual element to the ongoing search for Nessie, igniting public curiosity and inspiring further investigation.

In 1977, a photograph taken by Anthony Shiels purportedly showed a hump-like object moving through the water, resembling the classic image of the Loch Ness Monster. The photograph, known as the Loch Ness Monster Submarine Photograph, caused a stir among Loch Ness enthusiasts and sparked debates about its authenticity. Critics have questioned the photograph's validity, citing the possibility of a manipulated image or the use of a model submerged in the water.

It is important to note that the credibility and authenticity of these photographs have been subject to scrutiny and skepticism. While some of these images have become iconic representations of the Loch Ness Monster, their veracity remains a topic of debate. Hoaxes, misinterpretations, and the potential for misidentifications must be taken into consideration when examining the photographic evidence associated with Nessie.

These iconic photographs have left an indelible imprint on the Loch Ness Monster legend, fueling public fascination and inspiring ongoing investigations. Despite the controversies surrounding their authenticity, these images continue to evoke a sense of wonder and contribute to the enduring mystery of Nessie.

Next, we will delve deeper into the scientific investigations, eyewitness testimonies, and cultural impact surrounding the Loch Ness Monster. By examining the evidence, analyzing the history, and exploring the complexities of the legend, we strive to unravel the truths, dispel the myths, and shed light on the enigmatic creature of Loch Ness.

The authenticity and controversies surrounding the images associated with the Loch Ness Monster have been subjects of intense scrutiny and debate. While these photographs have captured public fascination and played a significant role in shaping the legend, their veracity has been questioned. In this section, we will investigate the authenticity and controversies surrounding the iconic images linked to the Loch Ness Monster.

The Surgeon's Photograph, taken by Robert Kenneth Wilson in 1934, is perhaps the most famous Loch Ness Monster image. However, in 1994, it was revealed that Wilson's photograph was a hoax. It was actually a small model of a creature attached to a toy submarine, crafted by Christian Spurling, the son-in-law of Marmaduke Wetherell, a man who had previously been involved in a Nessie hoax. Despite its debunked status, the Surgeon's Photograph had a significant impact on the legend, fueling belief and interest for many years.

The Loch Ness Investigation Bureau (LNIB) captured several photographs during their investigations in the 1960s. While these images gained attention in Loch Ness Monster lore, their authenticity remains a subject of debate. Some skeptics argue that the photographs depict ordinary objects, such as logs or waves, while believers contend that they show evidence of a creature. The interpretation of these images remains subjective, and no definitive proof of the Loch Ness Monster's existence has been derived from the LNIB photographs.

The Dinsdale Film, shot by Tim Dinsdale in 1960, shows a hump-like object moving through the water of Loch Ness. While the film footage itself remains an intriguing piece of evidence, the still image extracted from the film has faced scrutiny. Critics argue that the image is blurry and lacks clear details, making it difficult to determine the nature of the object. The authenticity of the Dinsdale Film still remains inconclusive, with some suggesting it could depict a mundane phenomenon rather than the Loch Ness Monster.

The Loch Ness Monster Submarine Photograph, taken by Anthony Shiels in 1977, purportedly shows a hump-like object in the water resembling the classic image of the Loch Ness Monster. However, skeptics have raised doubts about the photograph's authenticity, pointing out potential inconsistencies in the lighting, shadows, and perspective. Some argue that the photograph may have been manipulated or staged, while others believe it could depict a floating object or a wave.

It is important to approach these Loch Ness Monster images with a critical lens and consider the controversies surrounding them. The surge of interest in the creature and the desire for evidence has made the Loch Ness Monster susceptible to hoaxes, misidentifications, and exaggerated claims. Scientific investigations and advancements in image analysis techniques have allowed for a more thorough examination of these photographs, raising questions about their authenticity and reliability.

While these iconic Loch Ness Monster images have left a lasting impact on the legend and continue to captivate the public's imagination, their authenticity remains contentious. It is crucial to evaluate the evidence with a balanced perspective, considering the potential for manipulation, misinterpretation, and the inherent challenges of capturing definitive proof of an elusive and enigmatic creature.

Next, we will delve deeper into the scientific investigations, cultural impact, and ongoing search for evidence surrounding the Loch Ness Monster. By examining the complexities of the legend and analyzing the available evidence, we aim to separate fact from fiction and shed light on the enduring mystery of Nessie, the enigmatic creature of Loch Ness.

46

# Chapter 7: Sonar and Submersible Investigations

Scientific investigations in Loch Ness have been crucial in the search for evidence of the Loch Ness Monster and understanding the mysteries that surround the legendary creature. Over the years, researchers have employed advanced technologies, including sonar and submersibles, to explore the depths of the loch and shed light on the enigmatic phenomenon. In this section, we will explore the scientific investigations carried out in Loch Ness using sonar and submersible technology.

Sonar (Sound Navigation and Ranging) has been extensively used in Loch Ness to create detailed maps of the underwater terrain and search for potential anomalies. Sonar systems emit sound waves that bounce off objects in the water and return as echoes, allowing scientists to create visual representations of the submerged environment.

In the 1970s, Operation Deepscan employed multiple sonar devices to scan the loch. The goal was to detect any large underwater objects that could potentially be the Loch Ness Monster. The operation covered a significant portion of the loch and generated extensive data, but it did not yield conclusive evidence of a large unidentified creature.

More recently, modern advancements in sonar technology, such as multi-beam and side-scan sonar, have enabled researchers to create highly detailed maps of the loch's underwater topography. These advancements have provided valuable information about the geological features of Loch Ness, but they have not definitively resolved the mystery of the Loch Ness Monster.

Submersibles and Remote Operated Vehicles (ROVs) have played a vital role in exploring the depths of Loch Ness and conducting visual surveys of the underwater environment. These remotely operated vehicles are equipped with cameras and other sensing equipment, allowing researchers to capture images and videos of the underwater surroundings.

In the 1970s, the Loch Ness Phenomena Investigation Bureau (LNPIB) used a mini-submersible called "Viperfish" to explore the loch's depths. Although the Viperfish was primarily designed for scientific research, it did not yield any definitive evidence of the Loch Ness Monster.

More recently, advancements in ROV technology have allowed for more sophisticated exploration of Loch Ness. These underwater vehicles can capture high-resolution images and videos, providing researchers with a closer look at the underwater environment. ROVs have been used to investigate potential underwater caves, hidden crevices, and other features that could serve as hiding places for the Loch Ness Monster.

Another innovative technique used in Loch Ness is Environmental DNA (eDNA) sampling. eDNA refers to traces of DNA shed by organisms into their environment, such as skin cells, scales, or waste. By collecting water samples from

Loch Ness and analyzing the eDNA present in the samples, researchers can identify the species that inhabit the loch.

eDNA sampling has been employed to study the biodiversity of Loch Ness, including the presence of various fish species. While eDNA analysis can provide valuable information about the ecosystem, it has not yielded conclusive evidence of an unknown large creature residing in the loch.

Scientific investigations utilizing sonar and submersible technology have greatly enhanced our understanding of Loch Ness and its underwater environment. These advanced techniques have produced detailed maps, visual surveys, and valuable ecological data. However, in terms of the Loch Ness Monster, these investigations have not provided definitive proof of the creature's existence.

Next, we will explore the ongoing scientific research, analyze the data collected, and examine the complexities of the Loch Ness Monster phenomenon. By considering the scientific investigations alongside eyewitness testimonies and cultural impact, we aim to unravel the truths, dispel the myths, and shed light on the enduring mystery of Nessie, the enigmatic creature of Loch Ness.

Scientific investigations utilizing sonar, submersibles, and other advanced technologies have provided valuable insights into Loch Ness and the mysteries surrounding the Loch Ness Monster. However, these studies also have limitations and require careful interpretation. In this section, we will examine the findings, limitations, and interpretations of the scientific studies conducted in Loch Ness.

Sonar surveys of Loch Ness have revealed detailed maps of the underwater terrain, highlighting the geological features and topography of the loch. These findings have contributed to our understanding of the loch's formation, such as the presence of deep trenches, submerged cliffs, and underwater caves. Sonar data has also helped identify known species of fish and other aquatic life in the loch.

However, sonar technology has its limitations when it comes to studying the Loch Ness Monster. Sonar can only detect objects that reflect sound waves, and small or elusive creatures may go undetected. Additionally, sonar cannot provide conclusive evidence of the existence or non-existence of a large unidentified creature like the Loch Ness Monster. Sonar data interpretation is subjective, and anomalies detected in the data may have alternative explanations, such as debris or other natural features.

The use of submersibles and Remote Operated Vehicles (ROVs) has allowed researchers to conduct visual surveys of the underwater environment in Loch Ness. These tools have captured high-resolution images and videos, providing a closer look at the underwater features, such as submerged trees, rocks, and sediment layers. They have also helped identify potential hiding places or areas of interest for further exploration.

However, the findings from submersibles and ROV investigations in Loch Ness have not produced definitive evidence of the Loch Ness Monster. Interpretation of the visual data relies on subjective assessment, and various underwater features may be mistaken for unidentified creatures. The Loch Ness environment presents challenges for visual surveys, including poor visibility due to sediment and limited exploration capabilities in deeper areas.

Environmental DNA (eDNA) sampling has been used to study the biodiversity of Loch Ness and identify the presence of various species. Through eDNA analysis, researchers have detected the DNA of known fish species that inhabit the loch, providing valuable insights into the ecosystem.

However, eDNA sampling has its limitations in studying the Loch Ness Monster. The method cannot conclusively determine the presence or absence of a large unidentified creature. eDNA analysis can only detect DNA traces of organisms that are shed into the environment, and the absence of Loch Ness Monster DNA does not disprove its existence. Additionally, eDNA analysis may be influenced by water currents, dilution, and other factors that can affect the detection and identification of DNA traces.

Interpreting the findings of these scientific studies requires careful consideration and a balanced approach. While sonar, submersibles, and eDNA sampling have contributed to our understanding of Loch Ness, they have not provided definitive evidence of the Loch Ness Monster. The absence of conclusive proof does not necessarily mean the creature does not exist, as the Loch Ness environment poses challenges to scientific investigation.

Furthermore, interpretations of the data collected can vary. Skeptics argue that the absence of compelling evidence supports the notion that the Loch Ness Monster is a myth or misidentification. Believers, on the other hand, maintain that the lack of definitive evidence does not negate the possibility of an elusive creature residing in the loch.

Next, we will delve deeper into the ongoing scientific research, explore the eyewitness testimonies, and analyze the cultural impact surrounding the Loch Ness Monster. By considering the data, limitations, and interpretations, we strive to shed light on the complexities of the legend and unravel the enduring mystery of Nessie, the enigmatic creature of Loch Ness.

# CHASING LEGENDS: THE TRUTH BEHIND THE LOCH NESS MONSTER

# Chapter 8: Cryptozoological Explanations

Cryptozoology is a field of study that focuses on the investigation and search for creatures whose existence is disputed or unverified by mainstream science. It explores the existence of cryptids, which are creatures that exist outside the realm of known zoology and often possess extraordinary or legendary characteristics. The Loch Ness Monster is one of the most prominent cryptids in cryptozoology, captivating the attention of researchers, enthusiasts, and skeptics alike. In this section, we will introduce the field of cryptozoology and its relevance to the Loch Ness Monster.

Cryptozoology combines elements of biology, folklore, and cultural anthropology, seeking to gather evidence and investigate the existence of creatures that have not yet been recognized by scientific consensus. It often draws upon eyewitness accounts, local folklore, and anecdotal evidence as starting points for exploration. The field encompasses a wide range of cryptids, including creatures like Bigfoot, the Yeti, and, of course, the Loch Ness Monster.

The relevance of cryptozoology to the Loch Ness Monster lies in its quest to uncover the truth behind the legends and mysteries surrounding the creature. Cryptozoologists approach the Loch Ness Monster with an open-minded perspective, acknowledging the possibility that there may be unknown or undiscovered creatures inhabiting the loch. They aim to gather evidence, conduct investigations, and analyze data in order to shed light on the existence and nature of such cryptids.

Cryptozoology provides a platform for researchers and enthusiasts to explore the Loch Ness Monster phenomenon from a multidisciplinary standpoint. It encourages the examination of historical accounts, cultural context, eyewitness testimonies, and scientific data to develop a comprehensive understanding of the creature and its alleged presence in Loch Ness.

However, it is important to note that cryptozoology is often met with skepticism from the scientific community. Critics argue that the field lacks a rigorous scientific framework and relies heavily on anecdotal evidence and subjective interpretations. The Loch Ness Monster, in particular, has faced criticism due to the lack of conclusive evidence and the presence of hoaxes and misidentifications throughout its history.

Despite the skepticism, cryptozoology plays a significant role in keeping the investigation of cryptids, including the Loch Ness Monster, alive. It fosters a sense of wonder, curiosity, and exploration, pushing the boundaries of our knowledge and challenging established scientific paradigms.

Next, we will continue our exploration of the Loch Ness Monster phenomenon, considering the scientific investigations, cultural impact, and ongoing search for evidence. By delving into the complexities of the legend and examining various perspectives, including those of cryptozoology, we strive to unravel the truths, dispel the myths, and shed light on the enduring mystery of Nessie, the enigmatic creature of Loch Ness.

The Loch Ness Monster has sparked numerous speculative explanations, ranging from scientific theories to imaginative hypotheses. These speculations attempt to provide possible explanations for the existence of the creature, delving into the realms of surviving dinosaurs, undiscovered species, and other intriguing possibilities. In this section, we will explore some of the speculative explanations put forth for the Loch Ness Monster.

One of the most fascinating and widely debated explanations is that the Loch Ness Monster represents a group of surviving dinosaurs or a descendant of prehistoric marine reptiles. Proponents of this theory suggest that a creature such as a plesiosaur or a similar aquatic reptile could have somehow evaded extinction and found a habitat in the depths of Loch Ness. They argue that the remote and inaccessible nature of the loch could have allowed these creatures to remain hidden from human observation.

However, the surviving dinosaurs hypothesis faces significant challenges. The extinction of non-avian dinosaurs occurred around 65 million years ago, making it highly unlikely for any such creature to have survived and gone undetected for such a long period of time. Additionally, the environmental conditions and limited resources in Loch Ness would pose challenges for the sustained survival of large aquatic reptiles.

Another speculative explanation is that the Loch Ness Monster represents an as-yet-undiscovered species, possibly a large aquatic mammal or an unknown type of fish. Loch Ness is a deep, freshwater loch with an extensive network of underwater caves and hidden passageways, providing potential hiding places for elusive creatures. Proponents of this theory argue that the Loch Ness Monster may be a part of the existing biodiversity that has managed to evade scientific detection.

However, the absence of conclusive evidence and the extensive scientific investigations carried out in Loch Ness present challenges to the undiscovered species hypothesis. The limited resources and ecological conditions in the loch would make it difficult for a large creature to sustain itself without leaving more definitive traces or being captured on camera or sonar. The lack of confirmed sightings and the absence of verifiable physical evidence make it challenging to support this hypothesis with scientific certainty.

Speculative explanations also delve into psychological and perceptual factors that may contribute to the Loch Ness Monster sightings. Some propose that optical illusions, misidentifications of known objects, or psychological predispositions can play a role in creating the perception of a mysterious creature in the loch. These explanations suggest that the human mind may project patterns and forms onto ambiguous stimuli, leading to the interpretation of something extraordinary when faced with ordinary phenomena.

Psychological and perceptual factors can certainly influence how eyewitnesses perceive and interpret their observations.

# CHASING LEGENDS: THE TRUTH BEHIND THE LOCH NESS MONSTER

They may contribute to misidentifications or the creation of mythical narratives surrounding the Loch Ness Monster. However, these explanations alone do not address all the reported sightings and cannot account for all the evidence associated with the creature.

It is important to approach these speculative explanations with critical thinking and scientific scrutiny. While they ignite imagination and contribute to the ongoing discourse surrounding the Loch Ness Monster, they require empirical evidence and further investigation to validate or refute their claims.

Next, we will continue our exploration of the Loch Ness Monster phenomenon, considering the scientific investigations, eyewitness testimonies, and cultural impact surrounding the creature. By analyzing the available evidence and examining different perspectives, we aim to unravel the truths, dispel the myths, and shed light on the enduring mystery of Nessie, the enigmatic creature of Loch Ness.

60

# Chapter 9: Psychological and Cultural Interpretations

The belief in mythical creatures like the Loch Ness Monster is influenced by various psychological factors that shape human perception, cognition, and interpretation. These psychological factors play a significant role in how individuals perceive and interpret their experiences, contributing to the belief in and fascination with cryptids. In this section, we will examine some of the psychological factors that contribute to the belief in mythical creatures.

Humans have a natural tendency to recognize patterns and meaningful shapes in random or ambiguous stimuli. This psychological process, known as pattern recognition, can lead to the perception of familiar objects or figures, even when they do not actually exist. Pareidolia is a specific form of pattern recognition in which people see recognizable images, such as faces or animals, in unrelated or random visual stimuli.

In the context of the Loch Ness Monster, individuals may interpret ripples, floating debris, or waves in Loch Ness as evidence of the creature due to their predisposition for pattern recognition and pareidolia. The desire to perceive something extraordinary in everyday phenomena can influence people's interpretation of their observations, leading to the belief in the existence of the Loch Ness Monster.

Confirmation bias is the tendency to favor information that confirms one's pre-existing beliefs or expectations while disregarding contradictory evidence. In the case of the Loch Ness Monster, individuals who already believe in its existence may actively seek out information, anecdotes, or sightings that support their beliefs while dismissing or ignoring evidence that contradicts their perspective.

Confirmation bias can create a self-reinforcing cycle where individuals selectively interpret and remember information that aligns with their beliefs, strengthening their conviction in the existence of the creature. This bias can contribute to the perpetuation of the Loch Ness Monster legend and the formation of belief communities around it.

Belief in mythical creatures like the Loch Ness Monster is often influenced by cultural transmission and social influence. Cultural narratives, folklore, and media representations shape people's beliefs and perceptions of the world around them. The Loch Ness Monster has become deeply ingrained in Scottish folklore and popular culture, perpetuated through storytelling, books, films, and other forms of media.

Social influence, such as family traditions, peer discussions, and community beliefs, can also play a significant role in shaping individual beliefs. People's beliefs in the Loch Ness Monster may be influenced by the collective beliefs of their social groups, reinforcing the cultural significance and acceptance of the creature as part of their identity or shared experiences.

# CHASING LEGENDS: THE TRUTH BEHIND THE LOCH NESS MONSTER

Cultural factors also contribute to the belief in mythical creatures like the Loch Ness Monster. The cultural context in which individuals grow up influences their understanding of the world and shapes their beliefs about the existence of extraordinary beings.

Folklore and mythology play a significant role in shaping cultural beliefs and traditions. In the case of the Loch Ness Monster, Scottish folklore and tales of water creatures, such as kelpies or water horses, have provided a cultural foundation for the belief in a mysterious creature inhabiting Loch Ness. These narratives, passed down through generations, contribute to the perception of the loch as a place where mythical beings could exist.

The Loch Ness Monster legend has also become intertwined with tourism and economic interests. The creature's fame attracts tourists from around the world, eager to explore the possibility of encountering Nessie or participating in the search for evidence. The local economy relies, in part, on the Loch Ness Monster as a draw for tourism, leading to the perpetuation and promotion of the legend.

Tourism-related activities, such as boat tours, museums, and Loch Ness Monster-themed merchandise, contribute to the cultural significance of the creature and its presence in the local community. The economic interests tied to the Loch Ness Monster create a vested interest in maintaining the belief and perpetuating the legend.

Belief in mythical creatures like the Loch Ness Monster is influenced by a combination of psychological and cultural factors. Human cognitive processes, including pattern recognition and confirmation bias, can shape the interpretation of observations and reinforce existing beliefs. Cultural narratives, folklore, and social influences further contribute to the acceptance and perpetuation of the Loch Ness Monster legend. Understanding these psychological and cultural factors is essential in comprehending why individuals continue to believe in and be fascinated by the existence of such creatures.

Next, we will bring together the various aspects explored throughout the book to provide a comprehensive understanding of the Loch Ness Monster phenomenon. By examining the scientific investigations, cultural impact, and the interplay between belief and skepticism, we aim to shed light on the enduring mystery of Nessie, the enigmatic creature of Loch Ness.

Popular culture, including movies, literature, and other forms of media, plays a significant role in shaping public perception of mythical creatures like the Loch Ness Monster. These cultural artifacts and narratives not only entertain but also inform and shape the collective imagination, influencing beliefs and perceptions. In this section, we will examine the role of popular culture in shaping public perception of the Loch Ness Monster.

Movies and television have been instrumental in popularizing and perpetuating the Loch Ness Monster legend. From early cinematic adaptations to contemporary productions, filmmakers have used the allure and mystery of the creature to captivate audiences worldwide. Films like "The Private Life of Sherlock Holmes" (1970) and "Loch Ness" (1996) have featured the Loch Ness Monster as central plot elements, further embedding the creature in the public consciousness.

Television programs have also contributed to the cultural fascination with the Loch Ness Monster. Documentaries, reality shows, and investigative series dedicated to exploring the mysteries of the creature have attracted viewers and fueled public interest. These visual portrayals often blend scientific investigations with storytelling, perpetuating the allure and sense of wonder surrounding the Loch Ness Monster.

Literature has long been a platform for exploring the Loch Ness Monster phenomenon. Numerous books, both non-fiction and fiction, have been written about the creature, offering different perspectives, theories, and stories. Authors have tapped into the legend's potential for adventure, mystery, and the unknown, captivating readers and further entrenching the Loch Ness Monster in popular culture.

Classic works such as "The Loch" by Steve Alten and "The Enigma of Loch Ness" by Henry H. Bauer have delved into the Loch Ness Monster's mysteries from fictional and scientific angles, respectively. These literary works, alongside countless others, contribute to the richness of the legend and its enduring presence in popular culture.

The rise of the internet and social media platforms has provided new avenues for the dissemination and discussion of Loch Ness Monster-related content. Online communities, forums, and social media groups have allowed enthusiasts, skeptics, and researchers to connect, share experiences, and debate the creature's existence. The Loch Ness Monster has become a prominent topic of discussion, contributing to its continued relevance and public engagement.

Through viral videos, user-generated content, and online platforms, the Loch Ness Monster has gained further visibility and cultural significance. Social media influencers, vloggers, and content creators often explore Loch Ness and the creature, adding to the diverse range of perspectives and interpretations surrounding the legend.

Popular culture's influence on public perception of the Loch Ness Monster cannot be overstated. Movies, television, literature, and online platforms shape the narrative, imagery, and emotional connection to the creature, fueling fascination, belief, and curiosity. These cultural artifacts have the power to shape public perception, perpetuate the legend, and inspire new generations to explore the mystery of Nessie.

Next, we will bring together the various aspects explored throughout the book to provide a comprehensive understanding of the Loch Ness Monster phenomenon. By examining the scientific investigations, eyewitness testimonies, cultural impact, and the interplay between belief and skepticism, we aim to shed light on the enduring mystery of Nessie, the enigmatic creature of Loch Ness.

# CHASING LEGENDS: THE TRUTH BEHIND THE LOCH NESS MONSTER

# Chapter 10: Skepticism and Hoaxes

While belief in the Loch Ness Monster persists among many, skeptics present compelling arguments against the creature's existence. Skepticism serves as an important counterbalance to belief, promoting critical thinking, scientific inquiry, and the evaluation of evidence. In this section, we will investigate skeptics' viewpoints and their arguments against the existence of the Loch Ness Monster.

One of the primary arguments put forth by skeptics is the lack of conclusive evidence for the Loch Ness Monster. Despite decades of scientific investigations, eyewitness testimonies, and technological advancements, no definitive evidence, such as clear photographs, physical remains, or DNA samples, has been produced that irrefutably supports the existence of a large unknown creature in Loch Ness.

Skeptics contend that the absence of concrete evidence suggests that the creature is likely a product of misidentifications, hoaxes, and exaggerations. They maintain that extraordinary claims require extraordinary evidence, and until such evidence is presented, the Loch Ness Monster remains unsubstantiated.

Skeptics also emphasize the role of psychological and perceptual factors in the Loch Ness Monster phenomenon. They argue that human beings are prone to misperception, misinterpretation, and cognitive biases that can lead to the belief in extraordinary creatures. Optical illusions, misidentifications of ordinary objects, and pareidolia—the tendency to see patterns and meaningful shapes in random stimuli—can contribute to the perception of a mysterious creature in Loch Ness.

Additionally, skeptics point out that eyewitness testimonies are often subjective and can be influenced by expectations, cultural narratives, and social influence. They argue that the Loch Ness Monster legend has been perpetuated through folklore, popular culture, and social reinforcement, leading individuals to interpret their experiences in alignment with the prevailing myth.

Skeptics emphasize the lack of sustained scientific evidence to support the Loch Ness Monster's existence. They contend that the extensive scientific investigations, including sonar surveys, submersible explorations, and eDNA sampling, have failed to produce verifiable evidence of an unknown large creature residing in the loch.

Skeptics highlight the challenges posed by the environmental conditions of Loch Ness, such as poor visibility, underwater debris, and the limited resources available to support the survival of a large creature. They argue that the absence of sustained scientific evidence suggests that the Loch Ness Monster is more likely a product of mythology, misperception, and human imagination rather than a tangible biological entity.

# CHASING LEGENDS: THE TRUTH BEHIND THE LOCH NESS MONSTER

It is important to note that skepticism does not necessarily deny the possibility of unknown species or extraordinary creatures. Skepticism promotes critical thinking, the evaluation of evidence, and the application of scientific methodologies to explore claims. Skeptics argue that extraordinary claims require rigorous evidence and that the Loch Ness Monster, as a scientifically unsubstantiated claim, does not meet that threshold.

Next, we will bring together the various aspects explored throughout the book to provide a comprehensive understanding of the Loch Ness Monster phenomenon. By examining the scientific investigations, eyewitness testimonies, cultural impact, skepticism, and the interplay between belief and doubt, we aim to shed light on the enduring mystery of Nessie, the enigmatic creature of Loch Ness.

The Loch Ness Monster legend has faced its fair share of hoaxes throughout its history, with certain notable incidents garnering significant attention and impacting the credibility of the legend. Hoaxes involving fabricated evidence, staged sightings, and manipulated photographs have cast doubt on the existence of the Loch Ness Monster and contributed to skepticism. In this section, we will expose some of the most notable hoaxes associated with the Loch Ness Monster.

The Surgeon's Photograph, taken by Robert Kenneth Wilson in 1934, is perhaps the most infamous hoax related to the Loch Ness Monster. The photograph, depicting a small, long-necked creature in the water, was widely circulated and fueled belief in the creature's existence for many years. However, in 1994, it was revealed that the photograph was a hoax. Christian Spurling, son-in-law of Marmaduke Wetherell, a man previously involved in a Nessie hoax, admitted that the photograph was a fake, created by attaching a small model to a toy submarine.

In 1977, a hoax involving a film crew from Yorkshire Television added to the skepticism surrounding the Loch Ness Monster. The crew, led by Robert Rines, claimed to have captured footage of the creature using sonar and underwater cameras. However, it was later discovered that the footage showed a prop resembling a monster head from a film production. The hoax severely undermined the credibility of the Loch Ness Monster research conducted by the team.

In 2014, an image on Apple Maps generated excitement when it appeared to show a large creature resembling the Loch Ness Monster. However, it was quickly revealed to be a digital manipulation, created by an artist using image-editing software. The hoax highlighted the ease with which digital media can be manipulated and disseminated, raising skepticism about the authenticity of Loch Ness Monster sightings captured through digital platforms.

Notable hoaxes have had a significant impact on the credibility of the Loch Ness Monster legend. They have raised doubts about the authenticity of evidence, eyewitness testimonies, and photographic material associated with the creature. The exposure of hoaxes has led to increased skepticism among the general public, scientists, and researchers, challenging the credibility and scientific legitimacy of Loch Ness Monster investigations.

Hoaxes have tarnished the reputation of the legend, fueling accusations of sensationalism, misrepresentation, and perpetuation of a myth. They have reinforced the arguments put forth by skeptics, who assert that the absence of verifiable evidence and the prevalence of hoaxes indicate that the Loch Ness Monster is a product of human imagination, misidentifications, and deliberate deception.

The impact of hoaxes goes beyond immediate skepticism. They have also had long-term repercussions, making it more challenging to separate genuine evidence or sightings from fraudulent or staged claims. Hoaxes contribute to the atmosphere of doubt and uncertainty surrounding the Loch Ness Monster, affecting the overall credibility of the legend and its acceptance within scientific circles.

It is crucial to critically evaluate evidence and claims associated with the Loch Ness Monster, taking into account the history of hoaxes and the potential for deception. Scientific rigor, skepticism, and a commitment to evidence-based investigations are essential in navigating the complexities of the legend and determining the truth behind the Loch Ness Monster phenomenon.

Next, we will bring together the various aspects explored throughout the book to provide a comprehensive understanding of the Loch Ness Monster phenomenon. By examining the scientific investigations, eyewitness testimonies, cultural impact, skepticism, hoaxes, and the interplay between belief and doubt, we aim to shed light on the enduring mystery of Nessie, the enigmatic creature of Loch Ness.

# CHASING LEGENDS: THE TRUTH BEHIND THE LOCH NESS MONSTER

75

# Chapter 11: Loch Ness Monster in Popular Culture

The Loch Ness Monster has captured the imagination of authors, inspiring a wealth of literary works that explore the legend and the mysterious creature. From non-fiction accounts to fictional tales, literature has played a significant role in shaping the cultural perception and fascination with the Loch Ness Monster.

"The Loch" is a novel that combines adventure, mystery, and the supernatural as it delves into the Loch Ness Monster phenomenon. The story follows a marine biologist who embarks on a scientific expedition to Loch Ness, uncovering secrets and encountering the enigmatic creature. Through its gripping narrative, the novel weaves together scientific exploration, folklore, and suspense, adding to the rich tapestry of Loch Ness Monster literature.

"The Enigma of Loch Ness" takes a scientific approach to the Loch Ness Monster, analyzing the evidence and exploring various theories surrounding its existence. The book critically examines eyewitness accounts, scientific investigations, and cultural influences to offer a balanced perspective on the legend. It delves into the complexities of the phenomenon and provides a thought-provoking analysis of the Loch Ness Monster.

The Loch Ness Monster has made its way onto the big screen and television, captivating audiences with its mystery and allure. Films and TV programs have used the legend as a source of inspiration for thrilling stories and visual spectacles.

"The Private Life of Sherlock Holmes" features the Loch Ness Monster as a central plot element in a Sherlock Holmes adventure. The film presents a fictionalized account of the detective's encounter with the creature during an investigation in Scotland. While the portrayal takes creative liberties, it showcases the enduring presence of the Loch Ness Monster in popular culture.

"Loch Ness" is a film that revolves around an American scientist who travels to Loch Ness to debunk the myth of the monster. As she delves deeper into her investigation, she forms a bond with a local man and discovers the possibility that the creature may indeed exist. The film blends drama, romance, and the allure of the legend, exploring themes of belief and scientific inquiry.

The Loch Ness Monster has been a subject of artistic exploration, inspiring various forms of visual representation. Artists have sought to capture the mystery, beauty, and awe associated with the creature through their creative interpretations.

Artists have depicted the Loch Ness Monster through paintings and drawings, offering their own visions of the creature. These artistic representations range from realistic interpretations to more imaginative and abstract depictions, reflecting individual perspectives and styles.

Sculptors and installation artists have also explored the Loch Ness Monster in three-dimensional forms. Their creations range from lifelike sculptures to abstract installations, conveying the mystique and grandeur associated with the legend.

Artistic depictions of the Loch Ness Monster serve to evoke emotions, spark the imagination, and contribute to the visual narrative surrounding the creature. They offer a diverse range of interpretations, allowing individuals to engage with the legend on a sensory and aesthetic level.

Next, we will bring together the various aspects explored throughout the book to provide a comprehensive understanding of the Loch Ness Monster phenomenon. By examining the scientific investigations, eyewitness testimonies, cultural impact, skepticism, hoaxes, and the interplay between belief and doubt, we aim to shed light on the enduring mystery of Nessie, the enigmatic creature of Loch Ness.

The Loch Ness Monster legend has captivated the imaginations of people around the world for decades. Despite the absence of conclusive evidence, the fascination with the creature has endured, drawing enthusiasts, researchers, and curious travelers to Loch Ness. In this section, we will explore the factors contributing to the enduring fascination with the Loch Ness Monster.

The allure of the unknown is a powerful driving force behind the enduring fascination with the Loch Ness Monster. The mystery surrounding the creature, the vastness of Loch Ness, and the possibility of encountering an elusive, legendary being evoke a sense of wonder and curiosity. The desire to uncover the truth and unravel the mysteries of the Loch Ness Monster continues to captivate the human imagination.

The Loch Ness Monster has become deeply ingrained in Scottish folklore and cultural heritage. The creature is seen as part of Scotland's rich tapestry of myths and legends, contributing to its significance in the local community and the wider Scottish identity. The cultural attachment to the legend has fostered a sense of pride and ownership, perpetuating its prominence and keeping it alive in the collective consciousness.

The Loch Ness Monster legend has also become a significant driver of tourism and economic activity in the region. Loch Ness attracts thousands of visitors each year, drawn by the allure of the creature and the picturesque beauty of the area. The legend has given rise to boat tours, visitor centers, museums, and a range of Loch Ness Monster-themed merchandise, contributing to the local economy and sustaining the fascination with the creature.

The Loch Ness Monster has been extensively commercialized, with its image and story used in various forms of media, marketing, and merchandise. The commercialization of the legend has both positive and negative effects, influencing public perception and contributing to its ongoing prominence.

# CHASING LEGENDS: THE TRUTH BEHIND THE LOCH NESS MONSTER

The Loch Ness Monster has been a subject of numerous books, films, documentaries, and television programs. These portrayals, whether fictional or based on real investigations, have played a significant role in shaping public perception and fueling the fascination with the creature. The media and entertainment industries capitalize on the Loch Ness Monster's allure, offering engaging stories, thrilling adventures, and captivating visual representations.

The legend of the Loch Ness Monster has spawned a wide range of merchandise, from clothing and accessories to toys and collectibles. Visitors to Loch Ness can purchase souvenirs featuring the creature's image, reinforcing the cultural significance and commercial value of the legend. The tourism industry capitalizes on the creature's fame, offering Loch Ness Monster-themed experiences, tours, and accommodations.

The commercialization of the Loch Ness Monster raises ethical considerations. While it contributes to the local economy and supports tourism, it can also perpetuate myths, misrepresentations, and distortions of the truth. The line between entertainment and the preservation of the creature's cultural and natural heritage can be blurred, requiring a balance between commercial interests and responsible stewardship.

The enduring fascination with the Loch Ness Monster is fueled by its mystery, cultural significance, and the economic impact associated with its legend. The commercialization of the creature has both positive and negative effects, shaping public perception, supporting tourism, and creating a market for Loch

Ness Monster-themed products. It is important to strike a balance between the preservation of the legend's cultural heritage and the responsible use of the Loch Ness environment.

Next, we will bring together the various aspects explored throughout the book to provide a comprehensive understanding of the Loch Ness Monster phenomenon. By examining the scientific investigations, eyewitness testimonies, cultural impact, skepticism, hoaxes, artistic depictions, and the interplay between belief and doubt, we aim to shed light on the enduring mystery of Nessie, the enigmatic creature of Loch Ness.

# CHASING LEGENDS: THE TRUTH BEHIND THE LOCH NESS MONSTER

83

# Chapter 12: A Global Phenomenon

L ake monster legends are not unique to Loch Ness. Similar tales of mysterious creatures lurking in the depths of lakes can be found in various regions across the globe. These legends, often fueled by reported sightings and local folklore, contribute to the rich tapestry of cryptozoological mysteries.

Lake Champlain, located on the border between the United States and Canada, is home to the legend of Champ. Described as a serpent-like creature with humps on its back, Champ has been reported by numerous witnesses over the years. Sightings date back to the early 19th century, and efforts have been made to capture evidence through photography and sonar surveys. Despite the lack of conclusive evidence, the Champ legend continues to intrigue locals and draw curious visitors to the lake.

Okanagan Lake in British Columbia, Canada, is associated with the legend of Ogopogo. Similar to the Loch Ness Monster, Ogopogo is described as a long, serpent-like creature with humps or a series of humps. The legend of Ogopogo has been passed down through indigenous folklore and oral traditions. Numerous sightings have been reported, capturing public interest and inspiring investigations. While skeptics attribute the sightings to misidentifications or natural phenomena, the legend of Ogopogo remains a cherished part of local culture.

Lake Como, situated in the Italian Alps, is home to the legend of the Lariosauro. Described as a reptilian creature resembling a plesiosaur, the Lariosauro has been a subject of fascination for centuries. Sightings have been reported by locals and visitors, often describing a long-necked creature with flippers. Efforts to capture evidence through photography and sonar have been inconclusive, leaving the existence of the Lariosauro open to speculation and further investigation.

Lake Nahuel Huapi, located in the Patagonian region of Argentina, is associated with the legend of Nahuelito. Described as a large creature similar to a plesiosaur or a sea serpent, Nahuelito has been reported by eyewitnesses since the early 20th century. Sightings often describe a long-necked creature with humps or a serpentine body. While skeptics attribute the sightings to misidentifications or hoaxes, the legend of Nahuelito continues to intrigue locals and attract tourists to the lake.

These are just a few examples of lake monster legends from around the world. Similar legends and reported sightings can be found in other regions, such as Lake Tahoe in the United States, Lake Tianchi in North Korea, and Loch Morar in Scotland. These tales of lake monsters capture the human fascination with the unknown, bridging the gap between folklore, myth, and the possibilities of undiscovered creatures.

While scientific investigations often yield inconclusive results, the legends and reported sightings contribute to the cultural heritage of the regions and inspire ongoing exploration. The enduring fascination with lake monster legends reflects

# CHASING LEGENDS: THE TRUTH BEHIND THE LOCH NESS MONSTER

humanity's timeless curiosity and the allure of the mysteries that lie beneath the surface of our planet's watery depths.

Next, we will synthesize the various elements explored throughout the book, providing a comprehensive understanding of the Loch Ness Monster phenomenon and its broader implications. By examining the scientific investigations, eyewitness testimonies, cultural impact, skepticism, hoaxes, artistic depictions, the enduring fascination, and similar lake monster legends, we aim to shed light on the enduring mystery of Nessie, the enigmatic creature of Loch Ness, and the intriguing world of cryptozoology.

Lake monster legends from different regions share common themes and characteristics, reflecting the universal human fascination with the unknown and our desire to explore the mysteries of the natural world. While each legend has its unique cultural context, there are notable comparisons and similarities among them.

Lake monster legends often describe creatures that resemble mythical beings from folklore and mythology. The Loch Ness Monster, Champ, Ogopogo, Lariosauro, and Nahuelito are frequently described as serpent-like or resembling prehistoric reptiles such as plesiosaurs. These similarities evoke a sense of wonder and connect these legends to a larger tapestry of human imagination and mythical narratives.

Many lake monster legends have roots in local folklore and indigenous traditions. Indigenous cultures often have longstanding beliefs in water spirits or creatures that inhabit specific bodies of water. These beliefs are passed down through generations, contributing to the cultural significance and authenticity of the legends. The integration of these legends into local folklore helps preserve cultural heritage and strengthens the sense of identity within the communities.

Lake monster legends have become tourism magnets, attracting visitors from around the world. The legends are often tied to the identity and economy of the surrounding regions. The legends serve as a draw for tourists, leading to the development of related attractions, tours, and merchandise. The economic impact generated by tourism supports local businesses and communities, reinforcing the cultural significance of the legends and their continued prominence.

Lake monster legends have cultural significance beyond their commercial value. They contribute to the collective imagination, folklore, and identity of the communities associated with the lakes.

Lake monster legends ignite a sense of wonder and curiosity, encouraging people to explore the mysteries of the natural world. The legends create a sense of adventure and capture the human imagination, fostering a connection between people and the lakes they inhabit. The enduring fascination with these legends reflects humanity's innate curiosity and the desire to understand the unexplained.

Lake monster legends are deeply intertwined with local culture and heritage. They form part of the storytelling traditions, folklore, and oral histories of the communities. The preservation and continuation of these legends help safeguard cultural heritage, ensuring that traditional narratives and beliefs are passed down to future generations. The legends serve as a source of cultural pride and contribute to the identity of the regions they are associated with.

Lake monster legends reinforce the connection between people and their natural surroundings. The legends emphasize the importance of preserving the lakes and their ecosystems, as they are seen as habitats for these mythical creatures. This connection fosters environmental stewardship, encouraging people to appreciate and protect the natural world around them.

Lake monster legends have both commonalities and unique cultural significance within their respective regions. These legends evoke a sense of wonder, preserve cultural heritage, attract tourism, and promote a deeper connection to nature. They captivate the human imagination and reflect our ongoing fascination with the mysteries of the natural world.

Throughout this book, we have explored the Loch Ness Monster phenomenon and its broader implications. By examining the scientific investigations, eyewitness testimonies, cultural impact, skepticism, hoaxes, artistic depictions, the enduring fascination, and the comparisons to other lake monster legends, we have gained a comprehensive understanding of these enigmatic creatures. Through the lens of cryptozoology, we have delved into the boundaries between myth and reality, exploring the enduring mysteries that capture our curiosity and fuel our sense of wonder.

90

# Chapter 13: Modern Expeditions and Technological Advances

R ecent years have witnessed significant advancements in technology that have shaped Loch Ness Monster research. These innovations have enabled scientists and researchers to explore the depths of the loch and gather data in ways that were not previously possible.

State-of-the-art sonar and imaging technology have played a crucial role in Loch Ness Monster research. High-resolution sonar systems can create detailed maps of the loch's underwater topography, providing valuable insights into its geological features and potential hiding places for large aquatic creatures. Additionally, advanced imaging technology, such as multibeam sonar and side-scan sonar, has been utilized to capture detailed images of the loch's underwater environment, allowing for comprehensive surveys and data collection.

ROVs and AUVs have become indispensable tools in Loch Ness Monster research. These remotely controlled or autonomous vehicles are equipped with cameras, sensors, and sampling devices, enabling researchers to explore the loch's depths and collect data in real-time. ROVs and AUVs can reach areas that are inaccessible to human divers, providing a safer and more efficient means of investigation.

Scientists and researchers have conducted several recent expeditions and studies aimed at unraveling the mysteries of the Loch Ness Monster. These endeavors have employed advanced methodologies and yielded intriguing findings.

Led by a team of scientists from New Zealand, the Discovery of Loch Ness Project utilized environmental DNA (eDNA) sampling to search for evidence of the Loch Ness Monster. eDNA analysis involves collecting water samples and extracting DNA fragments left behind by living organisms. While the project did not find conclusive evidence of the creature, it did provide valuable insights into the loch's biodiversity, including the presence of various known species.

Operation Groundtruth, organized by Kongsberg Maritime, conducted a comprehensive survey of Loch Ness using advanced sonar technology. The survey aimed to create detailed maps of the loch's underwater features and explore potential habitats for the Loch Ness Monster. The data collected during the operation contributed to a better understanding of the loch's geological characteristics and provided a baseline for future studies.

Various ongoing monitoring programs and citizen science initiatives continue to contribute to Loch Ness Monster research. These efforts involve local communities, researchers, and enthusiasts collaborating to gather data, document sightings, and monitor the loch's ecosystem. The Loch Ness Project, led by the Loch Ness Centre & Exhibition, conducts year-round monitoring and data collection, fostering public engagement and scientific collaboration.

# CHASING LEGENDS: THE TRUTH BEHIND THE LOCH NESS MONSTER

As technology continues to advance, Loch Ness Monster research holds promising prospects for the future. Emerging technologies and methodologies, combined with increased collaboration among scientists, can further enhance our understanding of the loch and its mysterious inhabitant.

Advancements in DNA analysis techniques can help in studying the biodiversity of Loch Ness and identifying species present in the loch. Continued monitoring of the loch's water quality, temperature, and ecological changes can provide valuable data for assessing the viability of a large unknown creature residing in the ecosystem.

Continued development of remote sensing technologies, such as improved sonar systems and underwater imaging, can provide higher-resolution data and facilitate a more comprehensive exploration of the loch's depths. Innovative approaches, such as the integration of artificial intelligence and machine learning algorithms, may enhance the analysis and interpretation of collected data.

Recent expeditions and scientific advancements in Loch Ness Monster research have opened up new avenues for exploration and data collection. Technology, such as advanced sonar, ROVs, and AUVs, has enabled scientists to investigate the loch's depths with greater precision and efficiency. Ongoing monitoring programs and citizen science initiatives have fostered public engagement and collaboration, creating a collective effort in understanding the enigmatic creature of Loch Ness.

While the Loch Ness Monster's existence remains unproven, these advancements continue to contribute to our knowledge of the loch's ecosystem, biodiversity, and geological characteristics. As technology and research methodologies continue to evolve, the possibility of uncovering new insights and shedding light on the enduring mystery of Nessie remains an intriguing prospect.

Drones have emerged as valuable tools in Loch Ness Monster research, providing a unique vantage point and facilitating aerial surveys of the loch. These unmanned aerial vehicles offer several advantages for the search for evidence. Equipped with high-resolution cameras, drones can capture detailed aerial images and videos of Loch Ness. This enables researchers to study the surface of the loch, identify potential sightings or anomalies, and document the surrounding landscape. Aerial imaging also aids in the creation of comprehensive maps, enhancing the understanding of the loch's topography and potential creature habitats.

Some drones are equipped with thermal cameras that detect heat signatures. This technology can be valuable in identifying temperature anomalies in the loch's waters, potentially indicating the presence of large organisms or unusual thermal patterns. Thermal imaging helps researchers target specific areas for further investigation and supports the collection of evidence.

Advancements in DNA analysis techniques and environmental monitoring play a crucial role in Loch Ness Monster research.

These approaches offer new avenues for gathering evidence and assessing the biodiversity of the loch:

eDNA analysis has gained prominence in recent years as a non-invasive method for monitoring and detecting the presence of organisms in aquatic environments. By collecting water samples from Loch Ness, scientists can extract DNA fragments shed by living organisms, including potential creatures inhabiting the loch. DNA sequencing and analysis can help identify known species and potentially reveal the presence of previously unknown or undiscovered organisms.

Hydroacoustic monitoring involves using sound waves to survey underwater environments. Advanced hydroacoustic technologies, such as multibeam sonar and echo sounders, can generate detailed maps of the loch's underwater topography and identify potential creature habitats. These techniques help scientists locate and monitor areas of interest, contributing to a better understanding of the loch's ecosystem.

In addition to drones and DNA analysis, other emerging technologies are being explored in the search for Loch Ness Monster evidence. Innovations in underwater remote sensing technologies, such as underwater drones, advanced sonar systems, and submersibles, allow researchers to explore the depths of Loch Ness with increased precision and detail. These tools provide visual imagery, mapping capabilities, and real-time data collection, enabling researchers to investigate potential creature habitats and capture evidence.

Artificial intelligence (AI) and machine learning algorithms have the potential to enhance the analysis and interpretation of data collected during Loch Ness Monster research. By processing large datasets and identifying patterns, AI algorithms can aid in identifying potential sightings, analyzing sonar data, or even detecting anomalies in thermal imaging. Machine learning can assist in distinguishing genuine sightings from misidentifications or hoaxes, contributing to more accurate assessments of Loch Ness Monster evidence.

The integration of these cutting-edge technologies, including drones, DNA analysis, hydroacoustic monitoring, underwater remote sensing, and AI, holds promise for future Loch Ness Monster research. These technologies facilitate data collection, enhance analysis capabilities, and provide new insights into the loch's ecosystem. While the ultimate goal of uncovering conclusive evidence of the Loch Ness Monster's existence remains challenging, these advancements contribute to a more comprehensive and sophisticated approach to the ongoing search for answers.

Next, we will synthesize the various aspects explored throughout the book, providing a comprehensive understanding of the Loch Ness Monster phenomenon, its broader implications, and the evolving methodologies and technologies that shape the pursuit of evidence. By examining the scientific investigations, eyewitness testimonies, cultural impact, skepticism, hoaxes, artistic depictions, the enduring fascination, similar lake monster legends, and cutting-edge technologies, we aim to shed light on the enduring mystery of

# CHASING LEGENDS: THE TRUTH BEHIND THE LOCH NESS MONSTER

Nessie, the enigmatic creature of Loch Ness, and the intriguing world of cryptozoology.

# Chapter 14: Eyewitness Accounts and Personal Stories

The Loch Ness Monster legend has been fueled by numerous eyewitness testimonies over the years. While skeptics question the credibility of these accounts, there are individuals who passionately believe in their experiences.

Tim Dinsdale, a respected aeronautical engineer and Loch Ness Monster researcher, had a memorable encounter in 1960. He described observing a large, hump-shaped object moving through the water while filming it. Dinsdale's footage gained attention and sparked further interest in the Loch Ness Monster. His account, backed by his professional background and the recorded evidence, continues to be cited by believers as compelling support for the existence of the creature.

In 1933, George Spicer and his wife claimed to have witnessed a large, long-necked creature crossing the road in front of their car near Loch Ness. Their account, widely publicized at the time, helped popularize the Loch Ness Monster legend and generated curiosity and speculation among the public. Spicer's description of the creature as having a long neck and a small head contributed to the iconic imagery associated with the creature.

Alex Campbell, a respected journalist and hotel manager, reported a memorable sighting in 1934. According to his account, he observed a large, dark object moving across the water, leaving behind a noticeable wake. Campbell's reputation as a reputable figure lent credibility to his testimony, adding to the intrigue surrounding the Loch Ness Monster phenomenon.

Apart from these notable accounts, numerous individuals have shared their personal stories and experiences of Loch Ness Monster encounters. Many local fishermen and residents of the Loch Ness area claim to have encountered strange and unexplained phenomena while on or near the loch. They describe witnessing large, unidentified creatures, unexplained ripples or disturbances in the water, or peculiar behavior of wildlife. These personal stories, passed down through generations, contribute to the rich folklore and cultural heritage surrounding the Loch Ness Monster.

Tourists and visitors to Loch Ness often share their personal stories of potential Loch Ness Monster sightings. These accounts range from glimpses of large shapes or humps moving in the water to sudden disturbances or unexplained phenomena. While skeptics argue that these experiences may be influenced by the pre-existing belief in the creature, the emotional impact and conviction with which these stories are shared cannot be dismissed.

Eyewitness testimonies and personal stories play a significant role in shaping individual belief systems and the wider Loch Ness Monster narrative. These accounts, while subjective and open to interpretation, contribute to the enduring fascination and belief in the creature.

# CHASING LEGENDS: THE TRUTH BEHIND THE LOCH NESS MONSTER

Believers find validation in the sincerity, consistency, and reputation of the witnesses, considering their experiences as genuine encounters with the Loch Ness Monster. These personal stories add to the collective weight of the legend and strengthen the belief that there is an unknown creature residing in Loch Ness.

Skeptics, on the other hand, often attribute these accounts to misidentifications, hoaxes, or psychological factors such as pareidolia or expectation bias. They argue that the Loch Ness Monster phenomenon is primarily driven by cultural influences, folklore, and a desire for mystery and excitement.

Next, we will bring together the various aspects explored throughout the book to provide a comprehensive understanding of the Loch Ness Monster phenomenon. By examining the scientific investigations, eyewitness testimonies, cultural impact, skepticism, hoaxes, artistic depictions, the enduring fascination, similar lake monster legends, cutting-edge technologies, and personal stories, we aim to shed light on the enduring mystery of Nessie, the enigmatic creature of Loch Ness.

When examining eyewitness testimonies of Loch Ness Monster encounters, it is essential to consider the credibility of the individuals reporting these experiences. While credibility can be subjective and difficult to assess definitively, certain factors can be taken into account:

Eyewitnesses who possess a reputable professional background or are respected members of their communities may have higher credibility. Individuals like Tim Dinsdale, an aeronautical engineer, and Alex Campbell, a journalist and hotel manager, brought a level of credibility to their testimonies due to their established expertise and standing in their respective fields.

Consistency in the details of testimonies and corroboration from multiple witnesses can enhance credibility. When different individuals independently report similar observations or share corroborating evidence, it lends more weight to their accounts. This can be seen in cases where multiple eyewitnesses describe sightings with similar characteristics, such as the hump-shaped object or the long-necked creature.

Eyewitnesses who have no apparent personal gain or motivation to fabricate their stories are often viewed as more credible. When individuals do not stand to benefit financially, socially, or in any other way from their testimonies, it reduces the likelihood of deliberate deception or exaggeration.

Consistency within testimonies of Loch Ness Monster encounters is another aspect to consider when evaluating credibility. Consistency refers to the coherence and stability of details provided by multiple eyewitnesses or by an individual over time.

Consistency in the descriptions of the Loch Ness Monster, such as its size, shape, or behavior, can lend credibility to testimonies. When witnesses independently provide similar descriptions without prior knowledge of others' accounts, it suggests a genuine and shared experience.

Temporal consistency relates to the stability of details shared by eyewitnesses over time. If an individual's account remains relatively unchanged or consistent when shared over a significant period, it adds to the credibility of the testimony.

The absence of significant contradictions or discrepancies within testimonies enhances their credibility. Inconsistencies in essential details, timelines, or key observations may raise doubts about the accuracy or truthfulness of the accounts.

It is important to note that personal recollections can be influenced by various factors, including memory biases, cultural influences, and the power of suggestion. Therefore, even genuinely perceived experiences may contain inconsistencies or variations due to individual interpretation and cognitive processes.

In summary, assessing the credibility and consistency of eyewitness testimonies involves considering factors such as the reputation and professional background of the witnesses, consistency within accounts and corroboration from multiple sources, and the absence of personal gain or motivation. Evaluating these aspects can provide a framework for critically examining the testimonies and contributing to a more comprehensive understanding of the Loch Ness Monster phenomenon.

104

# Chapter 15: Loch Ness as a Tourist Attraction

The Loch Ness Monster legend has had a significant impact on tourism in the region surrounding Loch Ness. The allure of the mysterious creature has attracted visitors from around the world, resulting in economic growth and the development of various tourist-related activities.

The legend of the Loch Ness Monster has drawn countless tourists to the area, eager to catch a glimpse of the elusive creature or explore the scenic beauty of Loch Ness. The fascination with the legend has driven an increase in visitor numbers over the years, contributing to the local economy and tourism industry.

Boat tours are one of the most popular activities for visitors to Loch Ness. Tour operators offer guided excursions on the loch, providing visitors with the opportunity to explore its waters and learn about the legend. These tours often incorporate storytelling, historical information, and the chance to search for signs of the Loch Ness Monster, creating an exciting and memorable experience for tourists.

The Loch Ness Monster legend has led to the establishment of visitor centers and exhibitions dedicated to the creature. These centers provide information about the legend, scientific investigations, and the natural environment of Loch Ness. Visitors can learn about the history and cultural significance of the Loch Ness Monster, view exhibits, and engage in interactive displays, adding to their understanding and enjoyment of the legend.

The popularity of the Loch Ness Monster legend has spurred the development of various Loch Ness Monster-themed attractions and businesses catering to tourists' curiosity and fascination. The tourism boom around Loch Ness has resulted in the establishment of hotels, guesthouses, and accommodations catering to visitors. Many of these establishments incorporate Loch Ness Monster themes into their decor, creating a unique and immersive experience for guests. Additionally, restaurants and cafes in the area often offer Loch Ness Monster-inspired dishes and menus, embracing the legend as part of the local culinary experience.

The Loch Ness Monster legend has become a marketable aspect of the tourism industry, with an array of Loch Ness Monster-themed souvenirs and merchandise available for purchase. Visitors can find a wide range of items, including t-shirts, keychains, postcards, and plush toys, featuring the creature's iconic image. The sale of Loch Ness Monster merchandise serves as a source of revenue for local businesses and allows tourists to bring home a piece of the legend. The Loch Ness Monster legend has had a substantial economic impact on the region surrounding Loch Ness, benefiting local communities and the tourism industry.

The influx of tourists to the area has created employment opportunities, both directly and indirectly, in the tourism sector. Jobs in hospitality, tour operations, retail, and other related services have been generated, providing income and livelihoods for local residents. The increased tourism activity has boosted demand for local goods and services. Local businesses, such as food producers, artisans, and transportation providers, have benefited from the influx of visitors. This has created a multiplier effect, contributing to the overall economic growth of the region.

The Loch Ness Monster legend has incentivized the need for sustainable development and conservation efforts in the region. Recognizing the importance of preserving the natural environment and the legend's cultural significance, local authorities and organizations have prioritized initiatives aimed at environmental stewardship, habitat protection, and sustainable tourism practices.

In summary, the Loch Ness Monster legend has had a profound impact on tourism in the region surrounding Loch Ness. The allure of the legendary creature has attracted visitors from around the world, resulting in increased visitor numbers, the development of Loch Ness Monster-themed attractions, and economic growth for local communities. While the commercialization of the legend raises ethical considerations, the tourism industry has provided opportunities for employment, stimulated local businesses, and fostered the preservation of the area's natural and cultural heritage.

Next, we will bring together the various aspects explored throughout the book to provide a comprehensive understanding of the Loch Ness Monster phenomenon. By examining the scientific investigations, eyewitness testimonies, cultural impact, skepticism, hoaxes, artistic depictions, the enduring fascination, similar lake monster legends, cutting-edge technologies, personal stories, and the impact on tourism, we aim to shed light on the enduring mystery of Nessie, the enigmatic creature of Loch Ness, and the intriguing world of cryptozoology.

The Loch Ness Monster phenomenon has brought both economic benefits and potential drawbacks to the region surrounding Loch Ness. While the legend has contributed to the growth of tourism and the local economy, there are considerations and challenges that come with the commercialization and perpetuation of the phenomenon. The Loch Ness Monster legend has had several positive economic impacts on the region.

The legend has attracted a significant number of visitors to Loch Ness, leading to increased tourism activity. This influx of tourists has created employment opportunities in the hospitality sector, including hotels, guesthouses, restaurants, and tour operators. The tourism industry has become a vital source of income for local businesses and residents.

The popularity of the Loch Ness Monster legend has stimulated the growth of local businesses and the production of Loch Ness Monster-themed merchandise. Souvenirs, clothing, artwork, and other products featuring the creature's image have become sought-after items for tourists, generating revenue for local artisans and suppliers.

# CHASING LEGENDS: THE TRUTH BEHIND THE LOCH NESS MONSTER

The Loch Ness Monster legend has led to an increased focus on the preservation of the region's cultural heritage. Efforts have been made to document and interpret the legend, creating opportunities for cultural institutions and organizations to educate visitors about the history, folklore, and scientific investigations associated with the creature. These initiatives contribute to the preservation of the local cultural identity and heritage.

While the Loch Ness Monster phenomenon brings economic benefits, it also presents potential drawbacks and challenges. The commercialization and perpetuation of the Loch Ness Monster legend raise questions about authenticity and ethical considerations. The legend's popularity has led to the creation of hoaxes, staged sightings, and exaggerated claims, which can undermine the credibility of genuine research and eyewitness testimonies. Balancing the promotion of the legend with responsible and accurate information is essential to maintain integrity and ethical practices.

The increased tourism and human activity around Loch Ness can have environmental consequences. The construction of infrastructure, boat tours, and the accumulation of waste from tourism-related activities can pose challenges to the delicate ecosystem of the loch. Balancing tourism growth with sustainable practices and environmental conservation is crucial to protect the natural environment and its biodiversity.

The Loch Ness Monster phenomenon has created a seasonality factor in the tourism industry. The region experiences peaks and troughs in visitor numbers, with a significant concentration of tourists during the peak season. This dependence on seasonal tourism can lead to challenges in managing resources, employment stability, and maintaining year-round economic sustainability.

To mitigate potential drawbacks and maximize the benefits of the Loch Ness Monster phenomenon, various strategies can be implemented. Encouraging responsible tourism practices that promote environmental conservation, minimize ecological impact, and respect the local culture and heritage is crucial. This includes promoting sustainable tourism initiatives, educating visitors about the importance of the environment, and supporting local businesses that prioritize ethical and responsible practices.

Continued collaboration between scientists, researchers, and local stakeholders is essential. By conducting ongoing research, documenting eyewitness testimonies, and sharing findings transparently, the credibility of Loch Ness Monster research can be maintained. Encouraging open dialogue and critical analysis can help distinguish credible evidence from hoaxes or misinterpretations.

Developing a diverse range of tourism offerings beyond the Loch Ness Monster legend can help reduce dependence on seasonal tourism and provide a well-rounded visitor experience. Highlighting the natural beauty, cultural heritage, and other attractions in the region can attract tourists throughout the year, supporting a more sustainable tourism model.

# CHASING LEGENDS: THE TRUTH BEHIND THE LOCH NESS MONSTER

The Loch Ness Monster phenomenon has brought economic benefits to the region surrounding Loch Ness through increased tourism, employment opportunities, and the growth of local businesses. However, there are potential drawbacks such as authenticity concerns, environmental impact, and seasonal tourism dependency. By adopting responsible tourism practices, supporting scientific research, and diversifying tourism offerings, the region can maximize the benefits of the phenomenon while minimizing its potential negative effects.

Next, we will synthesize the various aspects explored throughout the book, providing a comprehensive understanding of the Loch Ness Monster phenomenon. By examining the scientific investigations, eyewitness testimonies, cultural impact, skepticism, hoaxes, artistic depictions, the enduring fascination, similar lake monster legends, cutting-edge technologies, personal stories, the impact on tourism, and the economic benefits and potential drawbacks, we aim to shed light on the enduring mystery of Nessie, the enigmatic creature of Loch Ness, and the intriguing world of cryptozoology.

112

# Chapter 16: Environmental and Conservation Perspectives

Loch Ness is not only renowned for its legendary creature, the Loch Ness Monster, but also for its environmental significance and natural beauty. The loch and its surrounding ecosystem support diverse flora and fauna, making it an important ecological and conservation area.

Loch Ness, with its deep waters and unique geological features, provides a habitat for a wide range of species, both in and around the loch. Its biodiversity and ecosystem are of significant ecological importance.

The loch is home to a diverse array of aquatic life, including various fish species, such as salmon, trout, and Arctic charr. These fish species support both recreational and commercial fishing activities, contributing to the local economy. Additionally, the loch's nutrient-rich waters sustain a complex food web, supporting other organisms such as invertebrates, amphibians, and water birds.

Loch Ness attracts a variety of avian species, particularly during the breeding season and migration periods. Waterfowl, such as ducks, swans, and grebes, can be observed on the loch, while surrounding wetlands and woodlands provide important nesting sites for a range of bird species. These avian populations contribute to the overall biodiversity and ecological balance of the area.

The immediate surroundings of Loch Ness encompass diverse terrestrial habitats, including woodlands, heathlands, and wetlands. These habitats support a wide range of plant species, provide shelter for wildlife, and contribute to the overall ecological health of the region. Protected areas and nature reserves around Loch Ness aim to conserve these habitats and the species they sustain.

Several conservation initiatives and organizations are actively involved in protecting the environmental integrity of Loch Ness. Various nature reserves and protected areas have been established to safeguard the ecological value of Loch Ness and its surroundings. These areas, such as the Loch Ness Special Area of Conservation and the Great Glen Special Protection Area, aim to preserve the diverse habitats, species, and geological features of the region. They provide opportunities for scientific research, habitat restoration, and public education.

Efforts are underway to restore and manage the habitats around Loch Ness to support native flora and fauna. This includes initiatives such as woodland restoration, invasive species management, and the creation of wildlife corridors. By improving habitat quality and connectivity, conservationists aim to enhance biodiversity and ensure the long-term viability of the ecosystem.

Education and awareness programs play a vital role in fostering a sense of environmental stewardship among local communities and visitors. Conservation organizations, visitor centers, and educational institutions provide opportunities for learning about Loch Ness's ecological importance, conservation challenges, and sustainable practices. Through guided tours, interpretive exhibits, and community engagement, these initiatives raise awareness about the need to protect and conserve the natural environment.

Sustainable tourism practices are crucial in maintaining the environmental integrity of Loch Ness. Promoting responsible visitor behavior is essential to minimize the environmental impact of tourism activities. Visitors are encouraged to follow guidelines on waste management, respect wildlife habitats, and engage in low-impact recreational activities. Responsible behavior helps preserve the fragile ecosystems around Loch Ness and ensures a sustainable future for the area.

Collaboration between the tourism industry and conservation organizations is vital for fostering sustainable practices. By working together, these stakeholders can develop tourism activities that are respectful of the environment, support conservation efforts, and contribute to the local economy. Sustainable tourism practices can generate economic benefits while minimizing negative impacts on the natural heritage of Loch Ness.

Loch Ness holds significant environmental importance due to its biodiversity and unique ecosystem. Conservation efforts, including the establishment of protected areas, habitat restoration, and environmental education, are essential in preserving the natural heritage of the loch and its surroundings. By promoting sustainable tourism practices and fostering collaboration between tourism and conservation stakeholders, the environmental significance of Loch Ness can be safeguarded for future generations to appreciate and enjoy.

By examining the scientific investigations, eyewitness testimonies, cultural impact, skepticism, hoaxes, artistic depictions, the enduring fascination, similar lake monster legends, cutting-edge technologies, personal stories, the impact on tourism, the economic benefits and potential drawbacks, and the environmental significance and conservation efforts, we have gained a comprehensive understanding of the Loch Ness Monster phenomenon and its broader implications.

The legend of the Loch Ness Monster has had a notable influence on conservation initiatives in the Loch Ness region. While the legend itself may be shrouded in mystery, it has sparked public interest and curiosity, drawing attention to the natural environment and ecological importance of the area.

The Loch Ness Monster legend has generated widespread interest and engagement from the public, both locally and globally. This increased awareness has translated into a heightened focus on the conservation of Loch Ness and its surrounding ecosystem:

The legend's popularity has provided a platform for educational programs and initiatives focused on the natural environment. Conservation organizations, visitor centers, and educational institutions have capitalized on the intrigue surrounding the Loch Ness Monster to educate visitors and locals about the region's biodiversity, habitats, and conservation challenges. By incorporating the legend into educational materials and activities, these initiatives have effectively raised awareness and fostered environmental stewardship.

The Loch Ness Monster legend has encouraged citizen participation in environmental monitoring and data collection. Public engagement through citizen science initiatives enables individuals to contribute to scientific research and conservation efforts. Loch Ness has become a focal point for enthusiasts and researchers alike, with individuals actively reporting sightings, collecting water samples for eDNA analysis, and documenting environmental changes. This collaborative approach strengthens community involvement and empowers citizens to play a role in conservation.

The intrigue surrounding the Loch Ness Monster legend has led to increased funding and support for conservation initiatives in the region. The tourism industry, fueled by the Loch Ness Monster legend, has generated revenue that can be directed towards conservation efforts. Tourism-related activities, such as boat tours, accommodations, and souvenir sales, contribute financially to conservation organizations and projects. This revenue stream supports ongoing research, habitat restoration, and environmental monitoring, enabling organizations to implement conservation measures effectively.

The Loch Ness Monster legend has attracted the attention of corporate sponsors and donors interested in aligning their brand with the mythical creature. Conservation organizations and research institutions have formed partnerships with businesses, both local and international, to support conservation efforts. These partnerships provide financial resources, expertise, and access to technology, furthering the capacity for conservation initiatives in the region.

The Loch Ness Monster legend has influenced habitat preservation and management strategies. The ecological importance of Loch Ness has been recognized through the establishment of protected areas and conservation designations. The legend's association with Loch Ness has amplified the need to safeguard its natural heritage, resulting in the creation of nature reserves, special areas of conservation, and special protection areas. These designations prioritize the conservation of critical habitats, species, and geological features, ensuring their long-term protection.

The allure of the Loch Ness Monster has driven ecological research and monitoring initiatives. Scientists and researchers, intrigued by the legend, have focused their efforts on understanding the loch's ecosystem and its biodiversity. The research and monitoring activities not only contribute to the understanding of Loch Ness but also provide valuable data for conservation planning and management.

The legend of the Loch Ness Monster has had a significant influence on conservation initiatives in the region. It has heightened public awareness, fostered engagement through citizen science, attracted funding and support from tourism revenue and partnerships, and spurred habitat preservation and management efforts. While the legend itself may remain enigmatic, it has served as a catalyst for conservation action, leading to the protection and preservation of Loch Ness's natural environment for future generations.

119

# Chapter 17: Scientific Perspectives

Scientific consensus on the existence of the Loch Ness Monster leans towards skepticism. After decades of investigations, the scientific community has not found conclusive evidence to support the existence of a large, unknown creature residing in Loch Ness. While acknowledging the possibility of unknown or undiscovered species in the natural world, scientists generally approach the Loch Ness Monster legend with a critical and evidence-based perspective.

Several factors contribute to the skeptical view:

1. Lack of Physical Evidence: Despite extensive searches, including the use of sonar, submersibles, and other advanced technologies, no definitive physical evidence of the Loch Ness Monster has been obtained. This absence of tangible evidence, such as biological samples, carcasses, or remains, challenges the existence of a large, unknown creature in the loch.

2. Eyewitness Testimonies: Eyewitness testimonies, often cited as evidence by Loch Ness Monster enthusiasts, are subject to various factors that can influence perception and memory. Human perception is fallible, and eyewitness accounts can be influenced by environmental conditions, misidentifications, hoaxes, or psychological factors. Skeptics argue that the reliability and consistency of these testimonies can be called into question.

3. Hoaxes and Misinterpretations: The Loch Ness Monster legend has been associated with several well-known hoaxes and deceptive photographs, such as the "Surgeon's Photograph." These incidents have eroded trust and credibility in photographic evidence and created skepticism around other supposed sightings and images. Hoaxes and misinterpretations have contributed to a climate of doubt surrounding the existence of the creature.

4. Loch Ecology and Environmental Constraints: Loch Ness's ecosystem poses challenges for the survival of a large, unidentified creature. The loch's cold waters, limited food resources, and depth make it less conducive to supporting a population of large, warm-blooded creatures like the Loch Ness Monster. The absence of viable ecological conditions for a large predator raises doubts about the sustainability of such a species in the loch.

While the scientific consensus leans towards skepticism regarding the Loch Ness Monster's existence, it is essential to note that science remains open to exploration and discovery. Scientists continue to approach the Loch Ness Monster phenomenon with an open mind, recognizing the possibility of unknown species or rare occurrences. Ongoing research and scientific investigations seek to gather verifiable evidence and shed light on the mystery of Loch Ness, regardless of the consensus.

Next, we will synthesize the various aspects explored throughout the book to provide a comprehensive understanding of the Loch Ness Monster phenomenon. By examining scientific investigations, eyewitness testimonies, cultural impact, skepticism, hoaxes, artistic depictions, the enduring fascination, similar lake monster legends, cutting-edge technologies, personal stories, the impact on tourism, the economic benefits and potential drawbacks, the environmental significance, conservation efforts, and the scientific consensus, we aim to offer a balanced perspective on the Loch Ness Monster mystery.

The viewpoints of reputable scientists regarding the existence of the Loch Ness Monster generally align with skepticism and a lack of belief in its existence. While individual scientists may have varying opinions, the prevailing scientific consensus leans towards a skeptical stance.

In 2018, Dr. Neil Gemmell, a geneticist from New Zealand, led a scientific study known as the "Environmental DNA Survey of Loch Ness." The study aimed to collect water samples from the loch to analyze environmental DNA and determine if there was evidence of any large, unidentified creatures. Dr. Gemmell's conclusion, based on the analysis, was that there was no conclusive evidence of the Loch Ness Monster.

Another prominent scientist with a similar name, Professor Neil Gemmell from the University of Otago, conducted a separate study in 2019 known as "The Loch Ness Project." This project involved a comprehensive search using environmental DNA sampling, sonar imaging, and satellite tracking. Professor Gemmell's conclusion echoed the skepticism shared by many scientists, stating that there was no evidence to support the existence of the Loch Ness Monster.

Dr. Charles Paxton, a statistician and biologist from the University of St Andrews, conducted a statistical analysis of Loch Ness Monster sightings in 2019. His research examined the reliability and consistency of eyewitness testimonies over the years. Dr. Paxton's findings indicated that the sightings were more likely the result of misidentifications, environmental factors, and the power of suggestion, rather than the presence of an unknown creature.

Dr. Adrian Shine, a marine biologist and director of the Loch Ness Project, has been studying Loch Ness for several decades. His research has focused on exploring the loch's ecosystem, investigating sightings, and providing scientific explanations for reported phenomena. While Dr. Shine remains open to the possibility of unidentified species, he maintains a cautious and skeptical stance, emphasizing the need for critical analysis and evidence-based investigation.

These reputable scientists, among others, have approached the Loch Ness Monster phenomenon with scientific rigor and critical thinking. While they acknowledge the allure and cultural significance of the legend, their conclusions are based on the lack of compelling evidence and the application of scientific methods to assess the credibility of eyewitness accounts and photographic evidence.

It is important to note that science remains open to exploration and discovery. Scientists continue to investigate Loch Ness, applying new technologies and methodologies, and are open to revising their conclusions should substantial evidence emerge. However, as of now, the prevailing scientific consensus leans towards skepticism regarding the existence of the Loch Ness Monster.

Next, we will synthesize the various aspects explored throughout the book to provide a comprehensive understanding of the Loch Ness Monster phenomenon. By examining scientific investigations, eyewitness testimonies, cultural impact, skepticism, hoaxes, artistic depictions, the enduring fascination, similar lake monster legends, cutting-edge technologies, personal stories, the impact on tourism, the economic benefits and potential drawbacks, the environmental significance, conservation efforts, the scientific consensus, and the viewpoints of reputable scientists, we aim to offer a well-rounded perspective on the Loch Ness Monster mystery.

126

# Chapter 18: The Future of Loch Ness Monster Research

The legend of the Loch Ness Monster has captivated the imagination of people around the world for decades. As technology advances and scientific methodologies continue to evolve, the future of research and investigations into the Loch Ness Monster legend holds several intriguing possibilities. Advancements in technology offer new opportunities for research and exploration.

Continued advancements in imaging technologies, such as high-resolution sonar, underwater drones, and remote sensing devices, can provide enhanced capabilities for exploring the depths of Loch Ness. These technologies can capture detailed images and data, allowing for more comprehensive mapping and analysis of the loch's underwater topography and potential biological activity.

The use of environmental DNA analysis has gained prominence in recent years. This method involves collecting water samples and analyzing the genetic material present in the environment. Future research may focus on utilizing eDNA analysis techniques to search for traces of DNA that could indicate the presence of unidentified species in Loch Ness. This approach has the potential to provide valuable insights into the biodiversity of the loch.

Advancements in aerial survey techniques, such as the use of drones equipped with advanced sensors and cameras, can facilitate detailed monitoring and mapping of the Loch Ness area from above. This can aid in the identification of potential habitats, geological features, and changes in the environment. Remote sensing technologies, including satellite imagery and LiDAR, can also contribute to a better understanding of the loch's landscape.

Further ecological studies can help in understanding the biodiversity, food webs, and ecological dynamics of Loch Ness. This research can shed light on the potential habitats and resources available for different species, including any unknown or undiscovered creatures that may reside in the loch.

In-depth geological and limnological investigations can provide a deeper understanding of the loch's formation, sediment composition, water chemistry, and hydrodynamics. These studies can contribute to our knowledge of the loch's ecosystem and its potential to support life.

If evidence of unidentified species in Loch Ness emerges, behavioral and population studies can help researchers assess their behavior, movement patterns, and population dynamics. These studies would provide valuable insights into the ecology and conservation needs of any new or unknown species that may be discovered.

Encouraging the public to participate in data collection through citizen science initiatives can significantly expand the reach and scope of Loch Ness Monster investigations. Enlisting the help of enthusiastic individuals, researchers can gather more data, including eyewitness testimonies, photographs, videos, and environmental observations, for comprehensive analysis.

Continued education and outreach programs are vital for fostering public interest and understanding of Loch Ness and its ecological significance. By providing accessible platforms for learning, such as workshops, seminars, and interactive exhibits, researchers can promote scientific literacy, critical thinking, and responsible engagement with the legend.

Engaging with local communities, including indigenous communities, and valuing their traditional knowledge can provide unique perspectives and insights. Collaborating with local residents, fishermen, and individuals who have a deep connection to Loch Ness can enhance research efforts and contribute to a more comprehensive understanding of the legend.

The future of Loch Ness Monster research and investigations holds exciting possibilities. Technological advancements, interdisciplinary collaborations, and public engagement can contribute to a more comprehensive understanding of Loch Ness and its mysteries. By utilizing advanced imaging technologies, conducting ecological and geological studies, and involving the public as citizen scientists, future research has the potential to shed new light on the legend and its underlying truths.

By examining scientific investigations, eyewitness testimonies, cultural impact, skepticism, hoaxes, artistic depictions, the enduring fascination, similar lake monster legends, cutting-edge technologies, personal stories, the impact on tourism, the economic benefits and potential drawbacks, the environmental significance, conservation efforts, the scientific consensus, the viewpoints of reputable scientists, and speculating on the future of research and investigations, we have provided a comprehensive overview of the Loch Ness Monster mystery and its multifaceted nature.

Advancements in technology continue to offer new possibilities for Loch Ness Monster research, promising to shed further light on the mystery. As researchers explore innovative approaches, several emerging technologies and methodologies hold the potential to enhance our understanding of Loch Ness and its legendary creature.

Autonomous Underwater Vehicles (AUVs) and Remotely Operated Vehicles (ROVs) equipped with advanced sensors and imaging technologies can facilitate detailed exploration of Loch Ness.

AUVs and ROVs can deploy high-resolution sonar systems to map the underwater topography of Loch Ness with greater precision. This technology can provide detailed images of the loch's features, enabling researchers to identify potential hiding places or unusual structures that may relate to the presence of unidentified species.

# CHASING LEGENDS: THE TRUTH BEHIND THE LOCH NESS MONSTER

Advanced imaging techniques, such as 3D sonar and laser scanning, can be employed to create detailed three-dimensional representations of the underwater environment. This can aid in the visualization and analysis of the loch's features, offering a more comprehensive understanding of its physical characteristics and potential habitats.

By collecting water samples from Loch Ness and analyzing the genetic material present in the environment, researchers can potentially detect DNA signatures of organisms inhabiting the loch. This approach could help identify and catalog the species present, including any unknown or undiscovered creatures.

eDNA analysis can provide insights into the biodiversity of Loch Ness by detecting and identifying DNA traces left behind by organisms. This non-invasive technique has the potential to reveal the presence of rare or elusive species, including those that may be associated with the Loch Ness Monster legend.

Satellite imagery captured using various spectral bands can reveal subtle changes in the loch's surface, such as temperature variations or the presence of algal blooms. Analyzing these data sets can aid in understanding the ecological dynamics and potential biological activity in the loch.

Utilizing thermal imaging technologies, such as infrared cameras or airborne sensors, researchers can detect variations in surface temperature that may indicate the presence of large organisms or unusual heat signatures. This non-intrusive approach could help identify potential Loch Ness Monster-related phenomena.

AI algorithms can be trained to analyze large volumes of visual data, such as photographs or videos, for the identification of patterns or anomalies. This technology can assist in sifting through the vast amount of Loch Ness-related imagery and identifying potential evidence or debunking hoaxes.

Big Data analytics can facilitate the integration and analysis of various datasets, such as environmental data, eyewitness reports, and historical records. By applying advanced data analytics techniques, researchers can uncover correlations, patterns, or trends that may provide insights into the Loch Ness Monster phenomenon.

It is important to note that while these emerging technologies and methodologies hold potential, they are not without limitations. Factors such as cost, accessibility, and environmental considerations may impact their application in Loch Ness research. Nevertheless, as technology continues to evolve, these approaches can contribute to a more comprehensive understanding of Loch Ness and its mysteries.

By examining scientific investigations, eyewitness testimonies, cultural impact, skepticism, hoaxes, artistic depictions, the enduring fascination, similar lake monster legends, cutting-edge technologies, personal stories, the impact on tourism, the economic benefits and potential drawbacks, the environmental significance, conservation efforts, the scientific consensus, the viewpoints of reputable scientists, speculation on the future of research and investigations, and emerging technologies and methodologies, we have provided a comprehensive overview of the Loch Ness Monster mystery and the tools that may help unravel its secrets.

# Chapter 19: Unexplained Phenomena and Mysteries

Beyond the enigma of the Loch Ness Monster, Loch Ness has been associated with various other unexplained phenomena and mysteries. The intriguing nature of the loch and its rich history have given rise to tales of strange occurrences and unsolved mysteries.

Reports of water vortexes and strange underwater currents in Loch Ness have intrigued both locals and visitors. Some eyewitness accounts suggest the existence of whirlpools and strong underwater currents in certain areas of the loch. These accounts describe peculiar water movements that cannot be easily explained by conventional factors, raising questions about the hydrodynamics and underlying geological features of Loch Ness.

Legends and theories propose the existence of underwater tunnels or hidden passages that connect Loch Ness to other bodies of water or subterranean networks. These tales speculate that the Loch Ness Monster and other mysterious creatures might use these hidden pathways to traverse different locations, adding to the mystique of the loch.

Loch Ness has been associated with sightings and experiences that defy conventional explanations. Several accounts describe the apparitions of phantom ships or ghostly vessels appearing and disappearing on the surface of Loch Ness. These sightings often occur under atmospheric conditions that create optical illusions, leading to speculation about paranormal or supernatural phenomena associated with the loch.

Reports occasionally mention sightings of strange lights or unidentified aerial objects (UFOs) hovering over or near Loch Ness. These accounts parallel similar phenomena reported in other locations, fueling theories of extraterrestrial activity or unexplained aerial phenomena associated with the loch.

Loch Ness has been linked to stories of time slips and historical anomalies, adding an element of intrigue to its lore. Some individuals claim to have experienced time slips or temporary shifts in which they find themselves transported to a different era while near Loch Ness. These accounts describe vivid encounters with historical scenes or individuals, creating a sense of crossing temporal boundaries within the vicinity of the loch.

Legends persist about lost treasures and hidden artifacts submerged in Loch Ness. These tales often involve ancient relics, valuable objects, or historical artifacts believed to have been intentionally hidden or lost in the loch's depths. Despite occasional searches, these treasures remain elusive, adding to the air of mystery surrounding Loch Ness.

While these additional unexplained phenomena and mysteries contribute to the allure of Loch Ness, it is essential to approach them with critical thinking and skepticism. Many of these accounts may be based on folklore, legends, or subjective experiences, and they often lack scientific evidence or corroborating testimonies.

Next, we will synthesize the various aspects explored throughout the book to provide a comprehensive understanding of the Loch Ness Monster phenomenon and the additional mysteries associated with Loch Ness. By examining scientific investigations, eyewitness testimonies, cultural impact, skepticism, hoaxes, artistic depictions, the enduring fascination, similar lake monster legends, cutting-edge technologies, personal stories, the impact on tourism, the economic benefits and potential drawbacks, the environmental significance, conservation efforts, the scientific consensus, the viewpoints of reputable scientists, speculation on the future of research and investigations, emerging technologies and methodologies, and other unexplained phenomena, we aim to present a well-rounded perspective on the mysteries and enigmas surrounding Loch Ness.

In addition to the Loch Ness Monster and other unexplained phenomena, Loch Ness has been associated with tales of strange occurrences, disappearances, and supernatural theories. These accounts add an element of mystery and intrigue to the already captivating lore surrounding the loch.

Some reports suggest the presence of magnetic anomalies in certain areas of Loch Ness. These anomalies allegedly interfere with compasses, navigational equipment, and even disrupt electronic devices, leading to peculiar experiences for those traversing the loch. These magnetic anomalies have been attributed to the unique geological characteristics of the region.

Loch Ness has been linked to accounts of time distortions and temporal anomalies. Some individuals claim to have experienced time lapses or distortions while in the vicinity of the loch, leading to disorientation, lost time, or encounters with historical figures. These tales fuel speculation about the existence of portals or other phenomena that disrupt the normal flow of time.

Over the years, there have been sporadic reports of individuals vanishing under mysterious circumstances near Loch Ness. While most of these disappearances can be attributed to accidents or other natural causes, a few cases remain unsolved. These unsolved vanishings have given rise to speculation about hidden dangers or inexplicable forces at play within the loch.

Loch Ness has long been associated with Celtic and Scottish folklore, which includes tales of water spirits, kelpies, and other mystical beings residing in the loch. Some theories propose that the Loch Ness Monster and other mysterious creatures are not physical creatures but rather manifestations of supernatural entities or guardians of the loch.

Ley lines, which are believed to be energy pathways that traverse the Earth, have been associated with mystical and supernatural phenomena. Some theories suggest that the ley lines intersect at Loch Ness, creating a convergence of powerful earth energies that influence the paranormal activities reported in the area.

# CHASING LEGENDS: THE TRUTH BEHIND THE LOCH NESS MONSTER

Loch Ness's rich history and association with ancient cultures have led to theories connecting the loch to occult practices or rituals. These theories propose that mystical or dark forces are at work in the region, influencing the Loch Ness Monster phenomenon and other unexplained occurrences.

It is important to approach these strange occurrences, disappearances, and supernatural theories with skepticism and critical thinking. Many of these accounts are rooted in folklore, legends, or subjective experiences and lack scientific evidence or verifiable testimonies. Loch Ness's mystical reputation and association with Celtic mythology may contribute to the creation of such theories, adding to the allure and enigmatic nature of the loch.

By examining scientific investigations, eyewitness testimonies, cultural impact, skepticism, hoaxes, artistic depictions, the enduring fascination, similar lake monster legends, cutting-edge technologies, personal stories, the impact on tourism, the economic benefits and potential drawbacks, the environmental significance, conservation efforts, the scientific consensus, the viewpoints of reputable scientists, speculation on the future of research and investigations, emerging technologies and methodologies, other unexplained phenomena, strange occurrences, disappearances, and supernatural theories, we have provided a comprehensive overview of the mysteries and enigmas surrounding Loch Ness.

# OLIVER LANCASTER

# Chapter 20: Conclusion

While the Loch Ness Monster remains elusive, the legend has had a significant cultural impact, attracting tourists, inspiring literature and art, and contributing to the conservation efforts in the Loch Ness region. Whether a mythical creature or a product of human imagination, the Loch Ness Monster legend continues to captivate the hearts and minds of those intrigued by the mysteries of the natural world.

The enduring allure and enigmatic nature of the Loch Ness Monster legend can be attributed to several factors that have captivated people's imaginations and sparked ongoing fascination.

The Loch Ness Monster represents a mystery yet to be fully unraveled. The allure lies in the possibility of encountering a creature that defies scientific explanation, stirring our curiosity and sense of wonder. The unknown and the potential for discovery fuel our imagination and keep the legend alive.

Loch Ness's association with ancient Celtic and Scottish folklore adds depth to the legend. The rich tapestry of mythical water creatures and tales of mystical beings in the loch's history taps into our fascination with ancient lore and legends, connecting us to a realm of magic and enchantment.

The Loch Ness Monster has become an integral part of Scottish and global culture. It is a symbol of Scotland's natural heritage and a source of national pride. The legend's widespread recognition and cultural significance have been reinforced through literature, movies, art, and popular media, keeping it embedded in our collective consciousness.

The human psyche is naturally drawn to mysteries and adventures. The Loch Ness Monster legend provides a sense of excitement and possibility, offering the allure of exploration and the potential for uncharted discoveries. It taps into our innate curiosity and desire for the unknown, satisfying our longing for adventure.

The Loch Ness Monster has fostered a strong emotional connection among believers and enthusiasts. The personal stories, eyewitness testimonies, and the belief in something extraordinary create a sense of belonging and shared experiences. The emotional attachment to the legend ensures its longevity and the continued search for answers.

Loch Ness, with its breathtaking landscapes and pristine waters, serves as a backdrop for the legend. The mystique of the loch enhances its appeal, drawing nature lovers and conservationists to appreciate and protect its fragile ecosystem. The Loch Ness Monster legend has indirectly contributed to the conservation efforts and sustainable management of the region's natural resources.

The enduring allure and enigmatic nature of the Loch Ness Monster legend lie in its ability to tap into our fascination with the unknown, ancient folklore, and the human desire for mystery and adventure. It represents a bridge between the realms of myth and reality, capturing our imagination and connecting us to the captivating mysteries of the natural world. Whether the Loch Ness Monster exists or not, its legend will continue to captivate and inspire generations to come, reminding us of the enduring power of myth, the allure of the unexplained, and our innate yearning for discovery.

Sign up to my free newsletter to get updates on new releases, FREE teaser chapters to upcoming releases and FREE digital short stories.

Or visit https://tinyurl.com/olanc

I never spam and you can unsubscribe at any time.

# Don't miss out!

Visit the website below and you can sign up to receive emails whenever Oliver Lancaster publishes a new book. There's no charge and no obligation.

https://books2read.com/r/B-A-UNEZ-QXQLC

**BOOKS 2 READ**

Connecting independent readers to independent writers.

# Also by Oliver Lancaster

Chernobyl: Unveiling the tragedy. A Comprehensive Account of the Nuclear Disaster

The Bhopal Gas Tragedy: Unraveling the Catastrophe of 1984

The Deepwater Horizon Oil Spill of 2010: A Disaster Unveiled

Fukushima Fallout: Unveiling the Truth behind the 2011 Nuclear Disaster

Minamata Disease: Poisoned Waters and the Battle for Justice (1932-1968)

Evil Women: Unmasking History's Most Notorious Women

Bundy The Dark Chronicles: America's Infamous Serial Killer

Dahmer The Dark Chronicles: America's Infamous Milwaukee Cannibal

Zodiac The Dark Chronicles: America's Infamous Cryptic Killer

Bigfoot: The Comprehensive Investigation into the Elusive Legend

Chasing Legends: The Truth behind the Chupacabra

Chasing Legends: The Truth behind the Loch Ness Monster

Watch for more at https://tinyurl.com/olanc.

# **About the Author**

Oliver Lancaster possesses an enchanting charm that effortlessly draws readers into the depths of his literary world. With an insatiable curiosity for the unexplained, he skillfully weaves tales of crime, conspiracy, mystery and the unknown, leaving readers on the edge of their seats.

Nestled away in the seclusion of his garden shed, Oliver finds solace and inspiration in the tranquility of nature. Surrounded by greenery and fragrant blooms, he dives into a realm of imagination, unearthing secrets that lie hidden within his mind.

Accompanying Oliver on his literary ventures is his faithful ginger cat named Italics. With his mesmerizing gaze and mysterious mannerisms, Italics adds an air of intrigue to Oliver's writing process, often curling up on a cushioned chair nearby, watching as words flow effortlessly from his human companion's pen.

When not engrossed in his craft, Oliver indulges in the gentle warmth of his garden with a glass of red wine.

Prepare to be spellbound as you delve into the pages of Oliver Lancaster's novels, for he is a master of the eerie, a weaver of secrets, and an unrivaled guide through the labyrinthine corridors of the human psyche.

Sign up to a free newsletter to get updates on new releases, FREE teaser chapters to upcoming releases and FREE digital short stories.

Read more at https://tinyurl.com/olanc.